An Invitation
From A
Catholic Godfather

An Invitation From A Catholic Godfather

*Seek God's will with a humble heart and believe in
His mercy and you will find your way to His truth*

Stephen Reidy

Mountain Crest
Publishing

Table of Contents

~~~~~~~~~~

Acknowledgments

Thanks be to God for His eternal goodness and love, for His gifts of creation, free will, and the grace necessary to accept the salvation offered through Jesus Christ.

Thanks to my wife Tryphena, who encouraged and supported me throughout this and really every project. She was my sounding board, first editor, advisor, and rock.

Thank you to two beautiful spirits, my mom and my dad for loving God first and living and sharing their faith.

Thank you to Fr. Terrence O'Connell, who has served as a loving example and guide in my spiritual life and whose feedback helped improve this book immensely.

Thanks to my friend and advisor Sue Gormley for her steadfast support, knowledge, and feedback on this endeavor.

Thank you to Sabrina Jean of FastTrack Editing for her generous support of this project. Her efforts and advice helped me grow as a writer.

Thank you to Elizabeth Leaver, whose finishing skills put the polish on my final draft. Her expertise was invaluable in helping me get to the finish line.

Thanks to Charlie and Conni Lawrence for their endless encouragement and feedback on the first draft. Their enthusiasm helped push me forward when I needed it most.

Thank you to my sister-in-law Carly Reidy for her feedback and advice as an early test reader. Her encouragement was a blessing on this journey.

Introduction

Fewer people than ever seem happy. They most likely don't realize that the emptiness they feel is a yearning for a stronger relationship with God. Following the will of God is oftentimes a struggle. Our corporal nature pulls us away from our spiritual nature, but it's the spiritual nature that leads to God and true happiness. The strategies to feed our spirit and draw closer to God start with knowledge and humility. God has been guiding humanity since ancient times, but we don't always slow down well enough to listen and really think about our choices. We rely on our conscience to provide on-the-fly guidance of right and wrong, but don't fully acquaint ourselves with what God has set before us. His word is beautiful and His plan for creation unparalleled, and we have the ability to choose our role in it.

Years ago I read a fascinating series of books in the Christian fiction genre. Through a remarkable event, many characters came to accept Christ and instantaneously never sinned, doubted, or questioned anything again. The storyline was interesting enough to keep me engaged, but the implausibility of the absolute and unwavering conversion of the characters, even under extraordinary circumstances, made it difficult to wholly relate to them. But it was fiction. In our world, with few exceptions, life doesn't work like that. Even most saints worked their way toward a full commitment to God.

Life is a journey, our shared journey. This book isn't the beginning or the ending of anything. It is just one step along a path that began when we were born and will end when we pass from this earthly life. The book is not about how holy we already should be; it's about how holy we really could be.

This invitation is not a substitute for a deeper dive into the love and knowledge of God's word through the Bible or church teaching, but a primer that stitches together a portrait of His love and plan for humanity using not just faith but also logic and reason.

Finally, a disclaimer before you read this book: I am a sinner. I don't want to be one, but I fail. I have repeatedly made poor choices and done the wrong thing, caring more for my own needs than loving my neighbor. I'm constantly working to reverse that pattern. Sometimes I feel as though I am taking one step forward and two steps back, but I know that if I keep trying, I can trust in the mercy of Jesus. So this book isn't about the mistakes I have avoided; it is about the mistakes I have made and the knowledge I have acquired through my own journey that I want to share.
God be with you!

To my Godchildren: Eric, Danielle, Anthony, Derek, Meaghan, and Carson,
You were my inspiration for this project. There is no treasure that I desire more for each of you than your eternal salvation. I pray that you will read this book with an openness to connect to its message and an understanding that it was written with love. Each of you is a gift from God and a blessing in my heart. I am eternally thankful for your presence in my life.

Finally to my children: Liam, Declan, and Owen, I love you more than you could know. I hope that in time, you will read this book thoughtfully and prayerfully, reflecting deeply on your choices and what they will mean in this life and in the next. May you keep your hearts ever open to the beauty of God's grace, and may His blessings forever rest in your souls.

Part One

Why Are We Here?

All Good Things Come From God

Chapter 1: The Purpose of Life

You have to be cautious with dreams and not allot more significance to them than they warrant. Sometimes, however, a dream is a technique our minds use to work through unresolved conflict. In my experience, a dream rarely provides a concrete resolution to a problem. But in many cases, I gain clarification, a fresh understanding, or a new perspective to consider.

Once, as I was attempting to discern the best possible path for my life, I had a dream. I was in a roofless stone arena with a huge winged demon flying slow, counter-clockwise circles around its perimeter. The creature was indescribably horrible and appeared in body as close to a dragon as anything else, but much more hideous. There was no love in it. Malice and an unnerving self-satisfaction emanated from the foul thing with a discernible stench that filled the entire arena. Its hide was black, not a color we have ever seen in our world but something much darker from which no light escaped, even from its piercing eyes. The monster flew in an unhurried manner, as though it were relishing the anticipation of claiming its prize as much as it enjoyed the actual devastation it would wreak when it did. I could see its loathsome awfulness without even looking at it, and the heavy sense of it permeated my consciousness. Under the shelter of the concourse, I had ninety minutes to decide on whether to choose God, or to choose to let this evil thing carry me off to hell. The choice was mine. While I mulled my options over, the wretched beast would periodically break its formation to claim a volunteer who stepped forward from beneath the concourse. Like lightning, it would strike with ferocity and speed. Clasping its human quarry in fearsome talons, the fiend would carry the poor soul off to hell. With each attack, I'd clench my teeth and take a breath as though the savage were striking my chest. As quickly as I would exhale, the vicious brute would be back to its slow circular pattern. I knew that as soon as I chose God, He would rescue or protect me. Still, I was waiting; pretty sure I would choose God but not wholly certain, and not ready to give up my remaining time. As aware of the consequences as I was, I wasn't overly worried, although I should have been.

When I awoke, I told my wife about the dream. She responded that the choice seemed pretty easy, and of course I must have chosen God. I replied with "yeah, you'd think so, but in the dream I was still considering which way to go." She was shocked.

Although the choice seems obvious, isn't it the same one that we are all making every day here on Earth, and one with equally dire consequences? When compared to eternity, our mortal life isn't even ninety minutes; it's the blink of an eye. The presence of evil in the choices we make may not be as self-evident as a blood-chilling creature, but the evil is there and the ramifications of choosing it are real. Even so, we delay or ignore the choice, as if our inattention isn't a choice itself.

When I think back on the creature specifically, the memory of it still has the power to give me a chill. Surprisingly, I wasn't afraid of it when I woke up. What I did fear was the propensity of my own human nature to consider choosing evil instead of good, even knowing the consequences. Now that I am awake, I am interested in deliberately considering the choices I must make. The point or purpose of this life is to make a choice.

Our culture continually conveys to us that you only live once (YOLO), so do whatever makes you happy and feels right for you. That motto is used to justify a range of choices from mostly innocuous actions, like eating another cupcake, to rationalizing much more reckless, dangerous, or sinful behavior. The inference is clear; the individual sets his or her own boundaries and is the ultimate arbiter of what should be done. He or she bases that judgment solely on what personally feels good. As a society, we have convinced ourselves that "being me" is the primary path to satisfaction and fulfillment.

The premise of the YOLO creed, however, is false because we actually live twice. The point of our first life is to freely choose which will be our second. The choice is not always an easy one. I'd like to imagine that if I were really in an arena, faced with the stark choice of safety or certain doom, I'd hit the escape hatch as quickly as possible. Unfortunately, the paths in this world that lead away from God are so numerous that they're not always easy to recognize. And on the surface, they are much more attractive than a flying demon. Plus, it takes work and self-sacrifice to get on the right path; work that, in many cases, souls are unwilling to undertake.

This glorification of self relies on an interior discernment of truth rather than a submission to the will of God. It's also predicated on the belief that we have value as humans because we are human, not because we were created by and in the image and likeness of God. Humans are the only visible creatures with the ability to know and love their creator and share in God's own life, and from this nature flows our dignity.[1] Believing that God created you solely for yourself is a very self-centered rather than God-centered view of creation. Humans were created to love and serve God and to offer all creation back to Him.[2] He must remain preeminent in your life. Accepting that truth, you must also accept that He requires something from you beyond occasionally thinking kindly about Him. You have to have more required of you than that.

God doesn't solely want us to be happy in this life. He wants us to love and honor Him first, no matter the cost. Growing up, my catechism book was titled *Know Him, Love Him, and Serve Him*. I still remember the green cover from one year and the brown from another. When you're a kid, you have lots of downtime, while adults busy themselves with whatever they think is important. They are always buzzing around in circles, shuffling papers and hurriedly speaking to one another. They still do it, and it leaves kids with plenty of time to wonder about the world around them. We'd have our CCD class and I would wonder, what does that title even mean? As a kid, I never figured it out. Maybe because I had so much downtime looking at the cover of the closed book, those words stuck with me and I never entirely ceased mulling them over. As an adult, I finally understood what now seems painfully obvious. The title was the formula or blueprint to reach and to please God.

That blueprint isn't perfectly linear, but the general order is important. You're not going to love someone you don't know. Maybe you will in a general way, but not in a specific way and not deeply. Which is the more painful loss: reading online that a drunk driver has killed someone, or having a police officer appear unannounced at your door to tell you that a drunk driver has killed a family member? You feel compassion and sorrow in the first case, but a deeply devastating grief in the second. A prayer and maybe a discussion with friends is most likely the extent of your actions on hearing the stranger's news. When a family member is the victim, your whole world changes. In time, most people are able to push through their grief. They learn to function and eventually feel happiness again, but the way in which they interact with the world will have been altered forever. The news will have changed their lives. Those different reactions are reflections of the different depths of love because, in the first case, they didn't really know the stranger. Our relationship with God is no different.

When you take the time to learn about God and get to know Him, you will begin to love Him more deeply. In your journey, that love will continue to mature as your knowledge does. Knowledge and love of God go hand in hand, but knowledge leads the way. Unfortunately, we seem to be skipping the first step, or certainly de-emphasizing the first one, and thereby diminishing the second. Knowledge is at an all-time low and an overemphasis on serving exists. Words without acts are empty, but acts without knowledge and love are fruitless. Serving God can lead to a deeper love of Him and happiness for you, but this service must have its roots in knowledge and love to be sustainable. You must start at the beginning.

Another readily available blueprint to which we can look for guidance on how to pursue a relationship with God is the Lord's Prayer. This prayer is recited so often that sometimes we can easily forget what we are saying when we pray it. There have been many books written on this prayer. That speaks both to its accessibility and to the depth of its meaning. The book in your hands isn't about the Lord's Prayer, so I will share a summarized version by highlighting four specific segments.

"Hallowed be thy name" is a command to keep the name of God and all that He is holy. We should approach Him with awe and wonder, and with a deep reverence born from that awe and wonder. That our reverence include an acknowledgment that He is far superior to us and perfect in every way is essential. We must approach God through holiness to grow more deeply in our understanding (know Him) of Him. That knowledge will lead us to a deeper love and a willingness to serve Him.

While "Hallowed be thy name" informs us how to approach God, "Thy will be done" uses four basic words to impart an unambiguous directive. The purpose of life is to make a choice, and simply stated, this is the choice: will we follow God's will, or will we follow our own? Everything else emanates from the answer to this question.

Many people think the purpose of life is mysterious, but it isn't. When seeking to do the will of God, there are many paths from which to choose. The mystery and complexity come in trying to choose one. Often our will and the will of God are not mutually exclusive, and remaining in unison with Him isn't always a conflict. Other times, even daily, our desires and wants may not align. Seeking to do the will of God isn't something to consider only when making a critical life-altering decision. Reflect on it frequently, in an attempt to ferret sin from your day and sinfulness from your nature, but do so with knowledge in order to discern correctly. When we pray "Thy will be done," it is an acknowledgment on our part that God's will should be done. We are also stating a willingness to conform our lives to His will, to ensure that it happens. We make this acknowledgment every time we pray the Lord's Prayer.

"Give us this day our daily bread" is a simple request from us to God to grant us the necessary knowledge and grace to discern His will in our lives. The fulfillment of this appeal in its most perfect form is manifested in the Holy Eucharist. The Eucharist is Christ's perfect sacrifice through which He pours His grace forth into our souls. It strengthens us in all spiritual gifts, and the more often we receive it, the stronger we become.

Souls can easily get caught up in daily life and begin to rationalize that a good person can pray at home to satisfy God's will and the individual's own needs. Aside from the reality that this excuse displeases God and violates the third commandment, it deprives the individual of the grace necessary to discern and do the will of God. The soul, like the body, must be nourished. Consider the effort expended in feeding the body. The gathering, prep, and cleanup time is immense, and it isn't something we do on our own. At times, we go to a restaurant, but even when we prepare food ourselves, we must seek help from another who grew or raised our food. The soul is infinitely more important than the body, yet so many have ceased to feed it. The Eucharist is food we cannot prepare on our own and imbues in us a gift we cannot receive in any other manner. "Hungry" is to our body, what "poor in spirit" is to our soul. Realizing that our own spirit is lacking or that we are poor in spirit is an important grace from God, and one for which we should pray.

We are bound by obedience to attend Mass weekly, and when in a state of grace (lacking any unconfessed mortal sins), participating in the Eucharist greatly strengthens us. Even when not receiving the Eucharist at Mass, being present and open to the word of God through the readings and homily work to strengthen and rejuvenate our souls. We've asked God to strengthen us daily, and while receiving the Eucharist daily may not be possible, there are other ways to receive strength to a lesser degree. You can pray at home, read the Bible, and use online resources on a daily basis to receive blessings and grace from God. These devotions should augment and not replace attendance at Mass.

The last portion of the Lord's Prayer that I want to highlight is "forgive us our trespasses as we forgive those who trespass against us." The message couldn't be much clearer. We are speaking a promise to God and agreeing to submit ourselves to the same judgment to which we hold others. When praying this line, really slow down and carefully think it through. Many people have errantly concluded that this portion of the Our Father is a "live and let live" clause, but that conclusion is entirely out of context. This promise is much more personal. It's not about people who are doing something somewhere that you may not like. This pledge is about people who've hurt you directly. Maybe the harm was committed as an unintentional slight, or maybe it was done with malice and forethought. Either case originates from a lack of love and attentiveness. Those shortcomings are also the ways in which we offend God. We cannot hurt God or lessen Him in any way, but we can offend and displease Him. When we do, how do we hope He responds to us? How have we responded to the people who have done that to us?

This covenant we make with God is a call to serve Him, by loving others the way He loves us. As easy as this pledge is to comprehend and even desire, it is sometimes so

17

difficult to do because we are fragile human beings. We feel and we hurt and we innately focus on ourselves. Shifting that focus to God and working to love others is really the culmination of knowing Him and loving Him and then serving Him. The Bible provides an illustration of when forgiveness received was not then extended to others.[3] Jesus told the parable of a servant who owed fifteen years' wages to the king. The servant couldn't pay and begged for forgiveness of the debt. The king, in his mercy, forgave the debt. The servant subsequently approached a second servant who owed the first one a day's wage. The second servant couldn't pay, so the first had him thrown in debtors' prison until he could. When the king learned of this behavior, he was angry because of the lack of mercy the first servant showed in a similar circumstance. He summoned the first servant, called him wicked, and threw him into prison until he could pay his debts. Christ then told the disciples, "So also my heavenly Father will do to every one of you, if you do not forgive your brother from your heart."[4] When I read that passage with a false sense of my own piousness, thinking that I would never do such a thing is easy. I'm not like that first servant at all. When I stop and read it with a humble heart, however, I can see in my own life, even as I write this, instances of my own unforgiving heart lacking in love for others.

Shifting the focus from us is so hard. To do so, we must approach God with awe, seek to do His will, ask for grace and knowledge, and treat all people with love–know Him, love Him, and serve Him. The formula is the same. From the book of Sirach: "Before a man are life and death, and whichever he chooses will be given to him."[5] This is the purpose of life: to make a choice and follow in Christ's footsteps. The next chapter outlines ideas on where to look for God and notes some common stumbling blocks that can impede that progress.

Chapter 2: Where Should We Look for God?

The best place to begin seeking an understanding of God's nature is through prayerful reflection and research. When in doubt about the best starting point for anything, always use prayer as your default position. To pray means to ask, and if you ask God, He will hear you, even if you don't feel as though you have nurtured a close relationship with Him. Attending Mass, reading the Bible, and reaching out to a priest or Godparent are all good places to build on your knowledge. Once you begin asking, you will find no shortage of people willing to offer their opinion, but they will not all be helpful on your journey. In fact, many will be openly hostile. Pray for those people, but avoid taking advice from them. One of my favorite quotes comes from St. Teresa Benedicta of the Cross: "Do not accept anything as the truth if it lacks love. And do not accept anything as love which lacks truth! One without the other becomes a destructive lie."[1] If someone is generally angry about you seeking a deeper relationship with God, they are working through their own challenges. Support them in any way you can, but search for spiritual nourishment in another direction.

Likewise, misinformation is rampant. Well-meaning and entirely sincere people will offer you information on God and what they believe to be true about His nature and will. The unfortunate reality is that countless people, including many Roman Catholics, are operating with errantly formed consciences. Their ignorance can be attributed to any number of reasons. Even with that caveat, an ill-formed soul will not lead you to a closer communion with Christ, but inadvertently away from Him. As well-meaning as these people may be, avoid their advice. The easiest way to identify someone who will reliably lead you toward the truth, is that you will hear them use phrases like "Well, the church teaches …," instead of "Well, I believe…." Humans are fallible beings with as many variants of interpretation of truth as there are people. God sent the Holy Spirit to guide His church on Earth precisely because of our divisive, proud nature, and because we could not possibly discern His truth without His support.

When questions of faith arise and you are uncertain about the correct church teaching, the *Catechism of the Catholic Church* is clearly written and 100 percent reliable. If you use only two books for your formation, the Bible should be one, and this should be the other. Recognizing the lack of a modern resource for lay Catholics to use in their faith formation, St. John Paul II gave us this clear, doctrinally correct text as an easily accessible reference. Those two books aren't the only ones that you will find useful in your formation; there are many. Works written by saints are an incredibly rich and underutilized resource for Catholic formation. Saints are often thought of as patrons of particular intentions, but they wrote deeply spiritual books that reflect a closeness to God worth emulating. Through their writings you can expose yourself to a much more God-centered way of ordering a life. Books about saints and how they lived are fascinating and humbling to read, but books authored by saints often provide insight into the thought processes and approach they brought to their faith. This point of view would be difficult to find through any other manner. Take advantage of the rich history and variety of authentic Catholic voices found in the writings of the saints, and you will gain a much better understanding of the whys and the context of church teaching.

You will find many hurdles along the way, challenges that test your faith. Some people fall down at the onset and struggle with accepting the existence of God. God exists and if you have ever doubted it, you should know that you are not alone. I'm not simply alluding to the hardened atheists who have convinced themselves that everything has randomly happened. Nor the agnostics who accept in general terms there may be higher intelligence somewhere in the universe, but nothing is known or could be known of such a being. I'm referring to ordinary, practicing Christians who also have questioned the existence of God. If you don't ask the question, how can you come to know the answer? Many people are born with an intrinsic sense that there is a God; I don't mean to insinuate otherwise. I am also not implying that they don't sincerely believe in God continuously throughout their lives. I am suggesting that even many of the people who fall into that category, at some point in their life, do some soul-searching about His existence. God calls all people to seek a deeper understanding and communion with Him as they grow. As Christians follow that innate call driven by a natural curiosity, they too must answer the existence question first.

Human beings, by their nature, are critical thinkers who constantly collect and process information in order to formulate judgments and make decisions. Think about the last time that you considered a major purchase. You most likely talked to friends and went online to review specs and learn from the experiences of other people who made a similar purchase. If you were in the market for a new home, you probably did research on lenders, crime rates, tax rates, schools, proximity to desirable amenities, and a host of other qualifiers. People do this investigation willingly because they have limited resources and want the best possible outcome. Consider that our time on Earth is the scarcest of all resources, and that the existence of God is the most important of all questions. God's very existence brings meaning and order to all other questions, yet many people spend very little time investigating His existence or His will.

We do seek Him though. We are wired for that. Looking for meaning in life, many don't realize that the answer lies with God. This lack of understanding makes getting distracted by a multitude of alternative options from the material world and substitute spiritualities very easy. None of these can fill the void left by the absence of nurturing a relationship with the one true God. This excerpt from St. Catherine's Dialogue succinctly expresses that principle: "Man is placed above all creatures, and not beneath them, and he cannot be satisfied or content except in something greater than himself. Greater than himself there is nothing but Myself, the Eternal God. Therefore I alone can satisfy him."[2] People who think they live without God, no matter how sincerely they hold their belief, don't live without Him any more than they live without oxygen to breathe. Both still sustain them. We now have scientific proof that oxygen molecules exist, and we have an understanding of exactly how oxygen sustains physical life. Prior to that discovery, humans recognized that there was something they couldn't see, measure, or fully understand that sustained their physical body. They knew it was there and they knew they struggled and died without it, but knowledge of its full nature eluded them. Likewise, God's existence doesn't depend on us to believe in Him. But unlike oxygen, His nature can never be fully understood by us. Consider these words from the *Catechism of the Catholic Church* as it quotes St. Augustine: "Even when he reveals himself, God remains a mystery beyond words: "If you understood him, it would not be God.""[3] His nature can be partially understood and He has revealed His truths to us through His word, His prophets, and most importantly, through the life and death of Christ.

While eighty-nine percent of U.S. adults continue to believe in the existence of God,[4] a growing subset of people feel that submitting to a belief in God somehow represents a diminished realization of their own intellect. At least some fear the perception of such from the standpoint of other people. They are embarrassed to openly proclaim a belief in God, and go to some lengths to make their belief seem unthreatening and not particularly strong. I recently attended a high school concert at which the song "The Prayer" was performed by a student and a teacher. The teacher introduced the song and explained that prayer is between God and a person. She then stammered through a further description, that prayer could be directed toward a higher being, between two people, or even to yourself. She told us this song could be thought of as spiritual, but she didn't think it was after considering it further. That's not a direct quote, but the gist of her message. She appeared uncomfortable and seemed as though she was making an excuse for singing something that was clearly a prayer to God. The song even asks for His guiding grace within the lyrics. Perhaps she was following the old adage and playing to her audience. The whole message left me confused about why she went through the explanation in the first place. An atheist connecting to that song in a way that would compel her to perform it is difficult to imagine, so why was she so self-conscious when speaking plainly about her faith in God? Could something in our shared culture have pushed us to be more reticent in professing a simple belief in God?

Some people want to believe in God but fear there is something wrong in doing so, and are afraid to commit. For them, God may not sound sophisticated enough to openly embrace. They're caught in a spiritual void and have morphed through different stages like "a higher being" and landed on "the universe" to describe the existence of a superior intelligence they know must exist. To feel discomfort ascribing intelligent power to a being but be willing to attribute it to an inanimate collection of stars and planets is an interesting dichotomy. We all studied the universe in science so perhaps speaking of its power rather than the power of God seems more socially acceptable. The truth is that when we turn away from God, we try to find something to fill the empty space we have created.

Today's world glorifies debate based on one-liners, memes, insults, and one-upmanship. The debate du jour regarding the existence of God has centered on the false principle that believing in God and embracing science are mutually exclusive. This idea has been repeated so often that many people no longer critically evaluate the argument; they merely accept it as truth. Accepting the fallacy of this proposition is only possible because so few people continue to believe that studying history is worthwhile. In the history of the world, this faux conflict is a fairly recent phenomenon, but is the most common impediment to believing in or expressing an open belief in God. Widespread acceptance of this premise has also caused Christians to be reluctant to unapologetically reveal their own belief in God. Reject the argument that God and science are mutually exclusive and don't be bound by it. Michael Coren wrote a book with a chapter specifically devoted to discrediting this myth. Among other evidence, he points to the following giants of science as devout Christians: Sir Francis Bacon, Johannes Kepler, Sir Isaac Newton, Robert Boyle, William Thomas Kelvin, Max Planck, Louis Pasteur, Alexander Fleming, Father Nicholas Copernicus and others.[5] His long list also includes Monsignor Georges Lemaitre, a Catholic priest and the father of the Big Bang theory. Monsignor Lemaitre was trying to explain how God created the world, and decidedly not attempting to replace God with some uncreated event to prove that God didn't exist. Incidentally, if a big bang was indeed the event that set in motion the aftermath that eventually led to life on Earth, two fundamental scientific problems still exist for the non-believer: where did the matter of the big bang originate (principle of mass conservation), and what set it in motion (causality)? Reflecting on these two essential questions for any length of time makes it unrealistic to deny the existence of God based on logic or reason.

In our own day, forty percent of working scientists believe in God[6] despite an enormous amount of pressure in their own community to treat science as their god instead. Plenty of definitions for science exist. Here is mine: Science is the manner through which the human race attempts to understand and explain how God created the world, how it works, and how everything within it interrelates. Admittedly, many scientists embrace the idea that the belief in God and the pursuit of scientific knowledge are mutually exclusive. Even so, their beliefs don't change the nature of what they are trying to understand.

God speaks to us in ways we can understand. Some of the Bible was written literally and must be interpreted that way, but not all of it. The USCCB teaches that "The Bible conveys the Word of God in many literary forms: historical narrative, poetry, prophetic exhortation, wisdom sayings, and novellas (edifying stories)."[7] In the Gospels, Christ often uses parables, and in other places there are stories to help the human mind grasp a concept. I've always marveled at arguments between atheistic scientists and literal creationists. The former stop at the first two chapters of Genesis and declare that there is no God. The latter believe that trying to fill in the blanks on how God created the world is somehow threatening or blasphemous. Neither camp approaches creation in the correct manner. Remember that God teaches us in ways we can comprehend. Genesis wasn't written to reveal cellular biology and the complexity of DNA and the genetic code because the people of that time couldn't have understood it. Thousands of years passed before humans got their arms around cellular biology, and hundreds more before DNA was understood in depth. DNA is complex beyond anything that we could have ever conceived, until we built continually on the knowledge of our predecessors. To write Genesis in a way that fully expounded on the complexity of God's creation was unnecessary, and would have been entirely ineffective to the ancient world. Genesis is history, not the foundation of scientific thought; recognizing that fact should not jeopardize our faith in the least.

With regard to creationism versus evolution, we are occasionally treated to televised debates on a cable pop science channel that pit an advocate from each side against the other. They bring their graphs, charts, quotes, pithy retorts, and a whole lot of passion. They're fun to watch, and both sides make interesting points. The trouble is that whole debate contains an undercurrent that to believe in evolution means to disavow God and His word. As a Christian, I am supposed to watch the debate, root for the creationist, and willingly walk away from God, if my side loses. Those alternatives are a false choice, and since I know what the church actually teaches, I don't get pigeonholed into buying into that fallacy. Pope Pius XII declared that the Church does not forbid us from believing in the doctrine of evolution in regard to our bodies coming from pre-existing matter but does require that we believe that God immediately creates souls.[8] Therefore, I can enjoy the debate and not worry about rooting for or against the existence of God. Does all of that mean that evolution is the way in which God created all life on Earth? No-but it doesn't preclude it.

Looking again at Genesis, we see the marking of days of time. Time does not even exist with God; He is infinite and not constrained by time. When we die, we likewise will no longer be constrained by time. On Earth, we mark time by the rotation of our planet on its axis and its journey around the sun. In the Book of Genesis there was no sun until the fourth day, so how were the first three days measured? The answer is that attempting to constrain God to our definition of time doesn't fit. Our inability to impose such a constraint upon Him should not cause doubt or concern on our part.

When some people come to Genesis, they approach it with a very literal and uncompromising understanding of time. In other books of the Bible, they would never interpret the text as literally and present it as the will of God. In the New Testament Christ told us "And if your right hand causes you to sin, cut it off and throw it away; it is better that you lose one of your members than that your whole body go into hell."[9] We would, in truth, be better off to lose a hand in this life than to lose our eternal salvation. But cutting off your own hand would be a grave sin and not what Christ was calling us to do. He was exaggerating the point that we should avoid the near occasion of sin. Maybe today He would say if your computer is the tool that leads you to sin, disconnect it and throw it away. That example is one way to apply that passage to life.

Misquoting and misinterpreting the Bible is not the exclusive realm of literally minded Christians; people unfamiliar with Scripture misuse it even more often. Leviticus 11:12 is continually misapplied during arguments in online forums. The verse prohibits eating shellfish, and people point to this universally unobserved dictate as proof that the Bible is fluid at best and untruthful fantasy at worst. This oft-repeated argument willfully or ignorantly disregards the difference between moral law, which cannot change, and ceremonial law that often does change. This quick quip is one of many used as an attempt to lead Christians off track. When you encounter such tactics, examine rather than accept them. They have all come up before and a more thoughtful review, by actual Biblical scholars, can be found at resources such as Catholic Answers or other online Catholic apologetics sites.

The science versus God debate misses an irony that science is often used to support a belief in the existence of God. An anonymous monk of the Maronite Monks of Adoration wrote a graphic novel using the pseudonym Amadeus. In it he asked, "Can the law of gravity explain why there's gravity in the first place?"[10] He correctly points out if there is a law, there must be a lawgiver. Laws of physics and mathematics likewise have not evolved. Consider again the complexity of DNA, the program of life. Shouldn't there be a programmer?[11]

Miracles are occurrences that cannot be explained by science or natural law. Instead, they can be observed and validated as outside of the natural law by science. Using science, they too can point to the existence of God. In 2014, a cult known as Raelians stole five consecrated Hosts from different parishes in North America and had them tested for DNA.[12] The Raelians committed this incredible sacrilege in an attempt to prove the Catholic doctrine of transubstantiation false through DNA testing. Unsurprisingly, the tests came back with evidence that the Host was in its physical essence, wheat. The results are unsurprising because either the Raelians misunderstood or misrepresented the church teaching. *Our Sunday Visitor's Catholic Dictionary* defines transubstantiation as "the change of the substance of bread and wine into the substance of the Body and Blood of Christ, so that only the accidents of bread and wine remain, when consecrated by a validly ordained priest."[13] That doctrine means the bread and wine turn into the Body and Blood of Christ, but their molecular makeup doesn't ordinarily change into human cells. The infusion of Christ's presence doesn't require that physical manifestation of the change. The Raelians desecrated the Holy Eucharist and purported to prove Catholic doctrine false, but actually accomplished absolutely nothing because they entirely misunderstood the doctrine. This misinformation is exactly the type of phony science you will run into when you begin to explore your faith more deeply.

The miracle of transubstantiation was not disproven in this case, but science was the conduit to prove the existence of Christ's body in the Eucharist in another case under very different circumstances. In the eighth century, a priest in Lanciano, Italy, doubted the real presence of Christ in the Eucharist. Upon consecration, he saw the bread and wine turn into actual flesh and blood on the altar before him. In 1971, Dr. Odoardo Linoli, a professor in anatomy, pathological histology, chemistry, and clinical microscopy, and head physician of the united hospitals of Arezzo, along with Dr. Ruggero Bertelli a professor emeritus of normal human anatomy at the University of Siena, examined the flesh and blood from the Lanciano miracle. They found the sample to be striated muscular tissue of the myocardium (heart wall) from a human with AB type blood.[14] The tissue was also found to contain no preservatives. The doctors observed that if the tissue had been taken from a cadaver, it would have deteriorated rapidly, yet it was perfectly preserved. The church has judged this miracle as worthy of belief. Through the ages there have been many miraculous healings and saints with stigmata that have been scientifically verified as unexplainable. The church doesn't require belief in these miracles, and basing your faith on them is ill-advised. God, through His grace, gives us miracles to encourage or awaken our faith, and we should accept and use them in that vein.

The fact is that for centuries the Catholic Church was the preeminent patron of science, universities, and healthcare. That, and her use of science to authenticate the existence of reported miracles, should put to rest the idea that science and God are somehow mutually exclusive.

I've presented ideas on where to seek God, and some of the most often encountered obstacles. The thrust of this chapter is neither to share every avenue of growth, nor refute every conceivable variation of attack. Instead, my intent is to encourage you not to lose heart at every arrow flung your way as you seek God. I also encourage you not to believe everything you hear about God, the Bible, or the Catholic Church. Approach your journey as I mentioned at the onset of this chapter, through prayerful reflection and research. Don't be dissuaded by people who don't make reaching heaven their priority, and don't believe everything you hear or read. This book is an invitation to delve deeper and learn more. Spend more time on this pursuit than on planning your next vacation or buying your next vehicle, and your reward will be much greater than those fleeting endeavors.

You will meet God, whether you believe in Him or not. How you want that meeting to go is something you need to decide now. This chapter covered some of the external roadblocks you will encounter, but the next will cover something much more difficult to conquer, and it comes from within.

Chapter 3: What Separates Us From God?

I used to be angry with Adam and Eve for the first sin. Through them sin and death entered the world. As a child, I imagined if only I had been there, I wouldn't have eaten of that tree and would have saved everyone a whole lot of heartache. Of course, even as a child, by the time I was mulling these views over in my mind, I had already done my share of sinning. As an adult, I look back on my naïveté and chuckle. Only a saint, completely sinless from the beginning, could make that claim. Our Blessed Mother Mary is the only human who fits into that category, which is why she is often referred to as the new Eve. By the grace of God, she was immaculately conceived, and when presented with an opportunity, made a different choice. In the beginning, God could have put Mary in the garden in place of Eve, but that was not His will.

Sin and rebellion entered the world when man used God's gift of free will to turn away from God's will. Many wonder why God didn't simply create us to live in love and follow His will, with no effort on our part. Why make things so difficult, why not put Mary and someone like her in the garden, why give us free will? The answer to that question is simple; without free will, love could not exist within us. Instead of living in love, we would live in servitude. Consider a despot who rules his country, allowing no freedom. The people must worship him as their dear leader and may never utter a word of disagreement with his platitudes, fearing threat of immediate death. Instead of being his children, the people are his slaves and hostages. His captives may express love out of duty, but it is not genuine and it is not love.

God wants His creatures to come to Him of their own free will. Think about your own life. Would you rather spend time and form a lifelong bond with someone because he or she freely chose to be with you, or because he or she was forced to be with you? The answer is the same with God. He desires humans to want to be with Him out of love rather than coercion.

Furthermore, God wants us to choose Him because we desire to be in His presence, and not because we do not want to go to hell. No one would want to be chosen like that. The Act of Contrition is an important prayer that Catholics use to express remorse for sins and resolve to love God more fully in the future. The Act of Contrition comes in many forms, but the one I have always used begins: "O my God, I am heartily sorry for having offended thee because I dread the loss of heaven and the pains of hell, but most of all because I have offended thee my God who art all good and deserving of all my love...." Many times I voiced those words without full sincerity. Even as I prayed them I recognized that mostly, I really just didn't want to go to hell. I knew hell was a bad place and it would be bad for me. In my mind, the ends justified the means, and as long as I eventually arrived in heaven, fearing hell and loving God were mutually acceptable paths. Self-love was my preeminent motivator. Like many, my obedience to God began out of a servile fear and not out of holy fear, which is the fear of offending God. The apostle John wrote in the Bible, "There is no fear in love, but perfect love casts out fear. For fear has to do with punishment, and he who fears is not perfected in love."[1] In this Scripture, John speaks of servile fear for one's own comfort and safety. He's not speaking of a holy fear that we should all nurture through a love of God and His virtues. Spiritual growth passes through many stages and there is nothing wrong with using servile fear as a starting point, as long as you do not become paralyzed by it. God speaking to St. Catherine of Siena told us, "It is true that, generally speaking, every person is first called in this way."[2] Her writings further elaborate that servile fear provides no protection against falling back into sinfulness, but holy fear and love of virtue for the love of God elevate the soul to a greater state of perfection.

As we advance in our faith we realize that we fear our own sinfulness and not Him. We come to understand how unworthy we are to be in His presence and serve Him, and perhaps fear that we may receive what we truly deserve. Then, something wonderful happens. We begin to develop a deeper knowledge of His nature and the truly unfathomable depth of His mercy. He is all-powerful. Yes, we are unworthy, but He loves us and wants us to be with Him anyway. In what human relationship can we conceive of such a love? Servile fear, which may always be present to some degree, will slowly give way to a love of God and a desire to be with Him. We should not allow the pace of the change to discourage us. God will accompany us on the journey and our goal is to increase in holiness, day by day. Few people have an instantaneous conversion experience through which they arrive at perfect love. When you read the writings of the saints, you will clearly see that they too struggled to conform their will to the will of God.

God's desire for us to love Him through His gift of free will is so essential, He didn't even rescind it when we used it to crucify His Son. Think about that for a minute to truly appreciate the depth of this gift. Christ walked among the people, and even then, God did not force them to worship Him. Many did, but many more did not and God permitted it to happen. People of our age often look for a sign or miracle, but when Christ Himself was with the people, their hearts still were not universally turned toward God. We are not being forced; we are being offered a choice.

Sin is the deliberate choice to do something other than God's will, and it is sin that separates us from Him; that uses our free will to choose to separate ourselves from Him. The whole purpose of our life is to follow God and conform our will to His; yet in some ways, we seem hard-wired to reject that, which seems paradoxical. We want what we want and what makes sense or feels right to us. This inconsistency only seems like a conflict when we look at sin through our eyes and not through the eyes of God. God knows better than we do what is good and best for us. When you hear people speak of trust in God, this truth is fundamentally what they mean. They trust in His goodness and the goodness of His law and the trials that He presents during our time on Earth. We can't understand why events don't always progress as we would have them progress, but when we mature in faith, we can learn better to accept it.

Rejection of God through sin is a process that often starts small and builds upon the separation. The further away from God's will a person "travels", the easier continuing on that path becomes. The momentum increases until eventually His call in a person's heart is wholly ignored. Most of the rationalization of sin falls into the category of "I'm not hurting anyone." In a YOLO, "if it feels good, then do it" culture, this reasoning seems to be a logical, rational thought. What it ignores is that all sin damages the sinner by putting distance between the sinner and God.

As humans, we want to be the arbiters of right and wrong and make those judgments in our consciences alone. We bargain, rationalize, de-emphasize, overemphasize, and generally find ways to develop a moral compass prejudiced by our own desires. We reject one that points to the true path set for us by God. We grant that distorted interior voice the power to reign over us, and adjust it periodically for our convenience. But a properly formed conscience is shaped with Scripture and divine teachings. The Holy Spirit does indeed speak to us through our conscience, but do not be fooled into thinking that voice is the only one we hear. Discernment takes work, and we achieve it through educating ourselves. Relying on feelings, rather than knowledge, is a perilous method of determining God's will because feelings are not rational, and feelings do not nullify truth.

Prayerfully centering decisions on the standard of what God wants, and not relying on personal desires, will lead to choices more in line with His will. Be wary if you find yourself thinking, "well, God wants me to be happy so this or that must be okay with Him." God indeed does want us to be happy, eternally in fact, which is why He provided His word through the Bible and the establishment of His church on Earth. We received His word first through the Law of Moses, and subsequently, through the life, death, and resurrection of Jesus Christ. Christ established the Catholic Church with Peter as its first head, to guide us in questions of truth. In the Nicene Creed, when we say we are an apostolic church, we are referring to the unbroken line of leadership, beginning with Peter and continuing to our current pontiff. Christ established a church on Earth to ensure that we could continually discern His truth and not rely on individual judgment.

God is truth[3] and God does not change,[4] thus His truth is not fluid. If left to the individual, the world would have as many versions of the truth as there are people. Consider what has happened since the Protestant Schism. What began as a small movement of men who disagreed with church teaching ultimately devolved into more than thirty thousand different protestant denominations, each with its own interpretation of the truth.[5] There can't possibly be that many versions of the truth. Broken down further to an individual level, the reality becomes clear that divine truth, determined by each individual, wouldn't be divine. Christ's church on Earth was established so that we would know the way to Him without the confusion or danger that comes from relying on personal revelation without His guidance. Truly, confusion comes from Satan and truth comes from God.

A common snare that runs counter to God, as the unchanging truth, is the belief that we are somehow more enlightened or more intelligent than people of past generations. The perception that for two thousand years Christians paid attention to sin and its consequences but that all of those people were wrong is false. Modern humans don't possess superior reasoning skills over the souls of the past who

35

rejected relative truth and believed in church teaching. The advanced state of our technology compared with that of the past is no indication of advanced intellect. Any reading of the doctors of the church or the great saints would put that bias to rest. The ancients, through more recent generations, shared our same proclivity for sinfulness and desire to bend the word of God to the will of man. We weren't the first to consider what God really intended. Of course they considered changing God's law, and until recent times, those changes were largely rejected. Now is a time in which many people believe creation is centered on the individual. The concept of encouraging people has morphed into the creation of "safe spaces" in which every idea is equally valid, and avoiding hurt feelings takes precedence over seeking truth. Even outside the safe space construct, an undercurrent of moral relativism has been cultivated as people look to their neighbors and think that their sins aren't as bad as their neighbor's sins. Sin is sin, and it separates us from the Father who created us in His image and likeness, to love and honor Him. How can something sinful be good? It can't; don't believe it.

Every sin, no matter how small, displeases God. St. Faustina had a vision of her own judgment on which she wrote: "I did not know that even the smallest transgressions will have to be accounted for."[6] Likewise, St. Catherine of Siena wrote of a vision of God in which He told her: "if one single sin were committed to save the whole world from Hell, or to obtain one great virtue, the motive would not be a rightly ordered or discreet love, but rather indiscreet, for it is not lawful to perform even one act of great virtue and profit to others, by means of the guilt of sin."[7] A parallel verse to this quote can be found in Proverbs: "Treasures gained by wickedness do not profit, but righteousness delivers from death."[8] So often, we are dismissive of what we believe are minor inconsequential sins. We lull ourselves into forgetting that God is perfect in His goodness and is the source of all life and holiness, and that even a minor separation from His love offends Him.

Minor or venial sins are "disobedience to God involving light moral matter or done without adequate knowledge, freedom, and full consent of the will."[9] Great attention is required to root out venial sins, primarily because they offend God, but furthermore, because they lead us away from virtue and toward more serious sinfulness. People believe that Judas Iscariot was some type of monster. He actually was just a man who let greed and pride lead him into darkness. If we recognize that we could travel down the same path, one sin at a time, we will be less likely to do so. Venial sin diminishes charity and merits temporal punishment, but doesn't eliminate the sanctifying grace necessary for salvation. A soul remits the temporal punishment of venial sin through prayer, fasting, almsgiving, and other holy works or sacrifices.

Mortal sin, on the other hand, completely separates a person from sanctifying grace. "It turns man away from God, who is his ultimate end and beatitude, by preferring an inferior good to him".[10] "For a *sin* to be *mortal*, three conditions must together be met: "Mortal sin is sin whose object is grave matter and which is also committed with full knowledge and deliberate consent.""[11] "Mortal sin... necessitates a new initiative of God's mercy and a conversion of heart which is normally accomplished within the setting of the sacrament of reconciliation."[12] "If it is not redeemed by repentance and God's forgiveness, it causes exclusion from Christ's kingdom and the eternal death of hell."[13]

These citations from the *Catechism of the Catholic Church* seem straightforward enough to stand alone. The difficulty surfaces when we internally attempt to discern the difference between mortal and venial sin. To say "I've never raped, robbed, or murdered someone and never will so I should be good" is easy. What about missing Mass on Sunday for something other than a serious reason, such as illness or the care of an infant? Missing Mass on a holy day of obligation falls into the same category. The *Catechism of the Catholic Church* is clear that both are grave sins.[14] As noted above, sin is a choice to put an inferior desire above the desire for God. Our weekly obligation to Him may be the most easily perceptible representation of that principle, yet many have never considered it that way. Fortunately, individuals do not own the burden of evaluating the seriousness of sins. The challenge comes in working to acquire the necessary knowledge to make sound moral decisions.

Have you ever heard someone say that if their pet isn't in heaven, then they don't want to go there either? That declaration is another obvious example of choosing an inferior creature to God. Christ Himself told us: "He who loves father or mother more than me is not worthy of me; and he who loves son or daughter more than me is not worthy of me."[15] Christ doesn't explicitly mention the family cat or dog, but He is clearly teaching that rightly ordered love puts God first without condition, even above family members. When people proclaim a disordered love that puts a pet above their love of God, they misunderstand a fundamental truth of God's love. The companion they loved so much was an extension of God's love to them, and not a love that existed in and of itself. All good things come from God,[16] including the creatures with which we share our lives. Without Him, they are lifeless, loveless, and meaningless. Pets are one small window into God's great love for us, but loving them more than loving God puts distance between a pet owner and God.

Those are just a few examples of sin. Everyone has their own particular sins with which they struggle-behaviors they know in their soul are wrong, but have convinced their minds couldn't possibly be sins and that God wouldn't really think of as important. They're the transgressions that we become accustomed to not fully examining or educating ourselves about because in our hearts we don't really want to know the truth. Then, instead of feigning ignorance, we'd have to acknowledge we were willfully disobeying God. Get to know all of your sins by examining your conscience on a regular basis. You can find useful lists online to help. Most run through the Ten Commandments with subcategories to facilitate a broader examination. You can even buy an app to examine your conscience, although I don't personally find entering sins into my phone exceptionally appealing or prudent.

Next, accept your sins and own them. Don't waste time manufacturing excuses or searching for extenuating circumstances that make you less culpable. None of those mitigating factors matter if you are truly sorry for your sins. Try to discover what leads you to bad decisions and eliminate or avoid it. A conversion of heart comes in really examining the difference between what an individual wants to believe and what God has directed through Scripture and divine teaching.

To truly unburden yourself, and in the case of any unconfessed mortal sins to return to a state of sanctifying grace, find a place where you feel comfortable going to the sacrament of reconciliation. If you are not in the habit of going, it may seem daunting. Rest assured, you are extremely unlikely to confess something to a priest that he hasn't heard before. I have been to confession many times, in different places and with different priests, and have never had a priest say to me that my sins were not forgiven. Nor have I heard of a priest saying that to anyone else. The sacrament is about reconciling sinners to the grace of God and welcoming them home. If you feel more comfortable going to a neighboring parish for greater anonymity, then do so. Feeling comfortable participating in the sacrament is better than avoiding it altogether. If you haven't been in a while, the priest will walk you through the process. Reconciliation isn't a stage show with an audience; it is you speaking to God through His representative on Earth. Christ instituted this sacrament[17] as a gift to His children as we continually fall and need reconciliation. Accept that gift and the peace that reconciliation and sanctifying grace bring. Christ died to redeem our sins; let

Him work through this sacrament to absolve you of them as well.

I've been fortunate to have an excellent confessor over the years. He has helped my spiritual growth immensely. In addition to administering the sacrament, he encourages me and shares advice on how I can continue to grow closer to God. Once, as I was struggling with one particular sin, he told me if I wanted to overcome it, I had to come to terms with its source. What caused it? Where did it come from? I left the confessional thinking that was great advice. Days later, I seemed no closer to an answer than when I had first heard the suggestion and was more annoyed than anything. He probably knew the answer-why not just give it to me? Why hold out? Months and several confessions later, I finally realized that specific sin was rooted in my own self-centeredness. I didn't love others as Christ taught; I loved my wants and me first. The answer should have been much easier to grasp and in retrospect seems painfully obvious. Most sin is rooted in self-love that becomes pride, crushing humbleness and blinding the sinner to its cause. When I finally told the priest that I had the answer, he was genuinely happy for me, and I appreciated why I had to work through the problem on my own. If I hadn't, I wouldn't have owned the solution. That is just one example of many in which my confessor has helped me.

This sacrament is available to you as well, and you can try different priests until you find a confessor that you feel comfortable with. Once you do, try to return to the same priest as often as possible. You will develop a relationship and most likely hold yourself more accountable knowing that you will be returning to the same confessor. Christ is really the man behind the curtain, so you are returning to the same confessor anyway. Our human perception sees the priest and so continuity will encourage you to cultivate virtue.

Now that we have covered the purpose of life, where we can find God, and what separates us from Him, it's time to consider the ramifications of using our free will. The next section covers why it matters, or from a human perspective, what's in it for me?

Part Two

What's In It for Me?

Jesus Christ Died for My Sins

Chapter 4: Salvation

When I was a boy, my parents took my brothers, sisters, and me to Good Friday services. Good Friday is the one day of the year on which Mass is not celebrated, but the church still holds a service. All of the priests attended and one, usually the youngest, would carry a life-sized cross upon his shoulder as he processed in. Part of the service consisted of the priests bellowing out the name of a sin and symbolically nailing a piece of paper to the cross with that sin written on it. Hearing words like pride, greed, lust, or envy followed by the echoing blow of the hammer as it came crashing down on the wood of the cross was startling. The list wasn't limited to the seven deadly sins; a multitude of misdeeds were acknowledged. Some priests approached the task with more verve than others and every blow would make me wince at the sound as I imagined the nails being driven into our Savior's hands and feet. The intent was to help us connect our sinful failings to the suffering of Christ and develop a deeper appreciation of all that He bore for us. The reverberation of the hammer seemed especially loud because the people, all of them, would sit in total, reverent silence, reflecting on the sins in their lives that brought everything to this point. Lent, and Good Friday in particular, is a time of great renewal and fresh opportunities to amend our lives. The symbolic nailing seemed a fitting culmination of the type of contrition that can transform a heart.

As a child, I would listen to the hammer strikes and wonder how many were directly attributable to my sinfulness. Surely there were worse people than me who accounted for more than my share. I'd start my list with murderers and eventually work my way up to Adolf Hitler before deciding I wasn't too bad of a guy. My sins probably only made Christ suffer a little compared to those of these other "big sinners" who weren't like me at all in the end. Even as children, pride

45

can lead us away from correcting our own faults and failings to focusing on the sins of others.

Now that the symbolic nailing of sins to the cross on Good Friday isn't done any more, I have heard people refer to the whole process derisively. For my part, I found great value in the exercise of publicly nailing sins to the cross and never stopped thinking about the experience. Well into adulthood I continued struggling to answer the question of how many blows of the hammer or lashes of the whip did Christ suffer because of my sinfulness. When I reached my thirties, I realized the answer was all of them. Christ died for the redemption of all, but He also died for the redemption of me. Jesus Christ died for my sins. If I were the only person who needed saving, He would not have suffered any less for me personally. That is true for you, too. Imagine loving an individual so much that you would suffer a torturous death over days to give that person life. For the first time, I fully understood what it meant to acknowledge Christ as my personal savior. I had to own every blow of the hammer and lash of the whip as coming from me just as I had to own the sinfulness of Adam and Eve as my own if I had been in their place. With that realization comes an acknowledgment of my own sinfulness and need to repent, but also joy in realizing the depth of love from the Creator of the world for me specifically. His love is incomprehensible to fathom.

Christ's self-sacrificial gift of love opened the passage to the never-ending happiness of full communion with God in heaven. Considering Christ's life and death from a human perspective, we may find ourselves questioning its necessity. Couldn't God simply have removed the stain of sin from man in some other way? The answer is of course He could have, but as St. Athanasius told us, "It is necessary, however, that we look to what was better for mankind, and not consider merely what was possible for God to do."[1]

God's plan is perfect and we must accept that He knows what is best, but we may naturally wonder why He chose reconciliation through the life and death of Christ. Consider this thought summarized from St. Catherine's writings: God is infinite and a sin against Him offends infinitely. In our finite nature we could not repair or redeem the bridge to God. In His mercy and love He united His own infinite nature to our finite human nature that through His sacrifice all of humanity could be redeemed.[2] Perhaps Christ's death was also done as the perfect example of obedience to demonstrate that there was no suffering that Christ would not endure to maintain alignment with the will of the Father. The best leaders of our world do not ask their followers to carry out tasks or endure trials that they themselves would not be willing to undertake. When Christ asks for our obedience, He has already shown us the way. Maybe His sacrifice was made out of compassion so that when we pray to Jesus, we would know He fully understands our hurts and our sufferings. Redemption through another method could conceivably have diminished the precious gift of free will. Greater theorists than I have written on this subject with more eloquence and depth. Whatever the reason, Christ's sacrifice was an act of perfect love of the Father in heaven through Jesus Christ, His Son. No greater love exists than to lay down a life for another. Christ's death was the perfect example of love and had to be such, because He is the perfect embodiment of love.

Understanding the difference between redemption and salvation is critical. Redemption is defined as "The deliverance of humanity from sin and the restoration of grace due to the passion, death, and resurrection of Jesus Christ. The redemption is God's free gift to mankind and cannot be earned."[3] Redemption unlocked the gates of heaven and it is a gift for all people.

Salvation is acceptance of the redemption offered through Christ's sacrifice. Salvation, like free will, is a gift, but unlike free will it can be rejected in its entirety. We may offer our will to the Father to guide us in whatever way He chooses, but even in this offering, the gift of free will remains with us. Christ died to redeem all people, but that does not mean that all people are saved. God told St. Catherine of Siena in one of her visions "though I created you without your help I will not save you without it."[4] Again, we see that the choice remains with the individual and it has real consequences.

Any decision to separate from God in this life is temporary, but without repentance will lead to a full and permanent separation in the next life, in a state called hell. That surely isn't a new idea, but it is one that many people, through indifference or lack of belief, give very little thought. Hell is one of the topics we all tend to look away from. As humans, we don't want to face anything so horrific. To comfort ourselves, we often consider the idea that maybe there is no hell or that only the worst of the worst find themselves there. We shudder to imagine the complete absence of God's presence. Yet instead of fully embracing Him in this life, we blot the ramifications of our actions out of our minds.

St. Faustina had a vision of hell, after which she remarked: "But I noticed one thing: that most of the souls there are those who disbelieved that there is a hell."[5] Intuitively, that makes a lot of sense. If people believed there was a hell and that they could wind up in it, wouldn't they do everything in their power to avoid such a fate? Conversely, if souls convinced themselves that a good God wouldn't create a place of eternal suffering and sorrows, they might not put much effort into seeking God's will in their life. The conviction that there is no hell could begin through poor formation, or creep in over the years through indifference or an unwillingness to amend habits that lead away from God's love. Perhaps ignoring the question altogether may seem more convenient, at least for the present time, and the soul could make an endeavor to sort it out later in life.

Hosts of people do not believe that hell exists. The thinking generally falls along the lines of how could a loving God condemn anyone to hell? But God does not condemn anyone to hell, for it is freely chosen, and people condemn themselves through their own sinfulness and rejection of God's mercy. Of the souls who do believe hell exists, a growing subset believes it lies empty, or at least there is some chance that no one or very few people have gone there. Without a consequence, however, everything we do in this life would be inconsequential. God didn't create us to have meaningless lives, nor did He create us to be robotic slaves. Hell has to exist for free will to exist, and as mentioned earlier, free will must exist for love to exist. To ignore the reality of hell is to deny the authenticity of love.

Christ Himself repeatedly affirmed the existence of hell and did so in explicit and unmistakable language, not the least of which was the parable of the rich man and Lazarus.[6] In it, Christ spoke of the torment and anguish of the damned and the eternal nature of the barrier between hell and those souls who died in God's friendship. In the Gospel, Christ referred to a place "where their worm does not die, and the fire is not quenched"[7] when speaking of hell, confirming again the eternal nature of the punishment. He also taught: "Enter by the narrow gate; for the gate is wide and the way is easy, that leads to destruction, and those who enter by it are many."[8] These are only a few of the several mentions of hell in Scripture. Many more examples can be found in both the New and Old Testaments.

Another perspective to reflect on is that of the saints who have been given visions of hell. It wasn't an empty warehouse waiting for that one unlucky soul who didn't quite make the grade. Unfortunately, hell was replete with souls, and the saints wrote of their torments in great detail. In His mercy, God allowed these visions to help us refocus on the truths of Scripture and divine teaching to usher us toward a proactive choice, rather than a selection through inaction.

49

Finally, we must consider other beings that we so often forget, the angels. The church has declared that some humans are definitely in heaven, but has never declared any particular human to be in hell. Any person who declared that another human was in or going to hell would be gravely presumptuous. Yet with angels, we know with certainty that some of them were cast into hell.[9] To believe that no human would condemn himself or herself to hell, but many angels did, seems fairly improbable considering their superior intelligence and perfect knowledge of God. I pray for everyone, even people who do grave evil in our time. I would love to believe that no one is in hell, but to believe so is harder than to believe not.

Hell can be difficult to entirely comprehend. St. John Bosco told us: "Our Lord always portrayed Hell in symbols because, had He described it as it really is, we would not have understood Him."[10] Christ speaks of a spiritual fire, and the term "burning" is used because it is the closest way in this world for us to understand. What occurs is a searing spiritual pain, a worm of conscience that never ceases eating away at its host. Primarily, the pain of hell is the eternal and complete separation from God. A secondary pain consists of the full knowledge of what has been lost, which was revealed in the instant of judgment. Worldly distractions and lies will no longer have the power to conceal the truth.

The exercise of free will does not always lead to the loss of salvation. On the contrary, it is intended to lead to the acceptance of the gift of salvation and the reward of eternal happiness. Jesus told His disciples: "In my Father's house are many rooms; if it were not so, would I have told you that I go to prepare a place for you?"[11] While hell is a complete and permanent separation from God, heaven is the full and permanent communion with Him. All of the beautiful people, pets, places, experiences, and anything else that brings joy in this life pales in comparison to the joy that could be yours for eternity in heaven. Science fiction books sometimes describe another dimension or a shadow world. It actually exists, but it isn't separate from this world; we are living in it. This Earth is a mere shadow of what it was created to be. The real world exists in heaven, where everything is conformed to God's will in perfect love.

While all good things come from God, they are temporary and will pass away, but God is infinite. He provides an infinite source of love and happiness to those who love Him. We have inadequate words and understanding to fully appreciate what a full and perfect union with God means. St. Paul told us, "What no eye has seen, nor ear heard, nor the heart of man conceived, what God has prepared for those who love him."[12] We read in Revelation, "God himself will be with them; he will wipe away every tear from their eyes, and death shall be no more, neither shall there be mourning nor crying nor pain any more, for the former things have passed away."[13] These are just a sampling of the many mentions of heaven in Scripture.

God desires all people to be saved,[14] and He continually waits for us to come home. In this life, we are never without His presence. The story of the prodigal son[15] is such a clear and loving example of God's goodness and generosity in welcoming back any sinner. People focus on the forgiveness of that story, but we should think more deeply about what is going on. That son believed he was living without the companionship of his father and was having a great time, or so he thought. His father made that life possible, but the son didn't acknowledge it, nor was he thankful. That ingratitude continued until the separation between the son and his father grew, and the son realized the emptiness of the path he was on. With no expectation of forgiveness, the son returned to his father and was welcomed in a way he never thought possible; he wasn't even sure that he would be welcomed at all. The prodigal son could have waited too long and died, alone, without the life-giving reconciliation that he found in his father's arms. That's the danger of living in sin. You may wait too long, and the separation may become permanent.

The insidious part of the story is that the prodigal son didn't initially realize what path he was on. Sin is like that. It starts as a gradual separation and becomes a chasm. The sinner creates so much distance that he begins not to listen *to* the voice of God, and then, fully stops listening *for* the voice of God. That is a much worse condition to be in and more difficult to return from. Draw near to God, now and always, and trust in His mercy to forgive.

Another son who is in the story is often forgotten. The elder son followed all of the rules without complaint, but his heart was lacking in charity. When his brother returned from his foray into the world, the elder son was bitter and jealous and refused to enter the house to be a part of the celebration. In loving mercy, the father reached out to the elder son and entreated him to join the festivities. He told the elder son that the father has always been with him and all that the father has, so too does the elder son. This beautiful father gave freedom and forgiveness and shared everything he had with his children. So too does our Father in heaven. Look for yourself in the story, and work to move away from the traits of the brothers and toward the love of the father.

This book won't cover purgatory in detail, but would be incomplete without its mention. When a soul dies in the state of mortal sin, he or she merits damnation. If a soul has repented and dies, either with venial sins present or the stain of sin present, he or she cannot immediately enter the presence of God. No sin can touch God and so the soul has to go through further purification. Those souls in purgatory will face no more tests and the path to God is irreversible, but they must be cleansed of their sin. Praying for the souls in purgatory is critical because they can no longer pray for themselves. Tim Staples of Catholic Answers has written a concise, easily digestible explanation of purgatory and looking it up would be well worth your time.[16]

Accepting the existence of hell and better understanding the nature of heaven may lead us into a servile fear. As discussed in the last chapter, this starting point is acceptable. St. Paul taught that we should "work out your own salvation with fear and trembling."[17] But don't do it alone. Parishes are a critical component to aid us on our spiritual journey through the sacraments and an increase in knowledge.

Parishes face an enormous level of pressure to fulfill their mission. In my parents' generation, and even when I was young, each parish had multiple priests serving the needs of the people. The parish of my youth had three resident priests and one rotating visiting priest to assist them. My city of forty thousand had three other parishes all with multiple priests, giving our local community more than a dozen priests in total. Now, many parishes have one priest and the less fortunate parishes have one they share with one or more other parishes. In addition to the challenge of being spread too impossibly thin to carry out all of the responsibilities they once did, many priests no longer have a community of their brethren in the rectory to serve as a social support network. Parish staff can be supportive and helpful but can never fully understand the priestly vocation. Nor can they be present when a tired priest retires to his home for the evening to offer a listening ear or an encouraging voice. Furthermore, older priests work well past secular retirement age because they know that there aren't enough seminarians to fill the current openings and don't want to exacerbate the problem by retiring.

The fact that many parents have turned over the development of their children's faith to religious education programs only increases the stress on a parish to deliver more services with fewer trained professionals. The reduction in resources has led to less consistency of message than there once was, and not all parishes are equally reliable partners in faith formation. Many have wonderfully welcoming mission statements in an attempt to be inclusive. However, when people join a parish, they are often never provided the message that they could lose their salvation or how that loss could happen. That lack of information won't help formation at all, and in fact, puts souls in jeopardy by lulling them into a false sense of security. In some cases, parishes stress that the two greatest commandments are to love God and to love your neighbors, but give little guidance on what that means beyond general service to others. They rarely, if ever, elucidate the particulars of precisely what constitutes mortal or grave sins.

In parish life you may see a general ignorance of the Catholic faith manifest in multiple ways. Misunderstanding salvation causes some people to immediately refer to the recently deceased as being in heaven. A great mercy of God is that He doesn't burden us with knowledge of the judgment of others. We should hope our loved ones are in heaven, but pray like they are in purgatory. If they are in neither of those places, we should leave that judgment where God has left it, in His hands. Sometimes, people go so far as to proclaim that their dearly departed has somehow transformed into an entirely different creature; an angel. The *Catechism of the Catholic Church* instructs: "As purely spiritual creatures angels have intelligence and will: they are personal and immortal creatures, surpassing in perfection all visible creatures, as the splendor of their glory bears witness."[18] On Earth, we sometimes imagine angels as a progression of our own spiritual development akin to the metamorphosis of a caterpillar into a butterfly, but it isn't so. No linear path exists between different types of creatures like humans and angels any more than there is a pathway between a cat and a dog. One will not transform into another. Angels aren't deceased human beings, and to say so demonstrates a misunderstanding of creation. Humans who enter heaven are instead considered saints. The church canonizes certain people who lived lives of extraordinary virtue. These canonized individuals pass many tests to be recognized as saints and are held up as examples for all the faithful to emulate, but they do not become angels. Souls who lived lives of ordinary charity are also considered saints once they reach heaven.

In parishes you may also meet people and hear about movements that attempt to bring about changes in church doctrine. Some Catholics don't agree with various tenets of the faith. The church though doesn't have the authority to change God's law; she is only the guide to help us understand and live in it.

You should still join a parish because you need the sacraments. Don't be confused if you encounter ignorance or misunderstanding of church teachings. Don't be discouraged if your parish isn't fully feeding your spiritual life or if you feel there are major pieces missing. Properly administered, their sacraments are still valid and you need those sacraments to fill you with the grace essential for salvation. Additionally, formation was never intended to be achieved solely through parish life. All parents have the responsibility to guide their children, and every person is responsible for himself or herself. Augment what's missing in your knowledge base with multiple other orthodox sources, remembering some of the suggestions from previous chapters. Also, attend Mass, but understand that showing up on Sunday and hobbling through the rest of the week outside of God's law is not enough. Christ told us Himself "Not every one who says to me, 'Lord, Lord,' shall enter the kingdom of heaven, but he who does the will of my Father who is in heaven."[19] Showing up, as they say, may be half the battle, but God is not satisfied with half measures.

Finally, believe the parish leadership when they preach about love, even if they do so exclusively. Love is indeed vital, but without knowledge, it may be misapplied and you may think of something as love that is not. In the next chapter, we will explore love in more depth, and it isn't always as self-evident as you may think.

Chapter 5: Love

People often speculate about dying in their dreams. Many of us have heard the frightening myth that if you die in your dreams, you die in your sleep. This narrative predates movies such as *The Matrix*, whose characters physically die in the corporal world if they don't make it out of the matrix alive. I have often wondered if the creator of *The Matrix* had the death/dream myth in mind when writing the script for the movie. Either way, it's not true because I died in my dream and lived to tell about it.

I'm not sure how I died, but my death was over before I knew it was happening and I found myself before Christ for judgment. He was sitting on a throne and our Blessed Mother was standing slightly behind Him off to the side. Oddly, I had no sense of standing or kneeling before Christ. I was simply present and unaware of any body.

Jesus told me that my judgment was hell. In the moment of delay between the time I learned of my judgment and had it carried out, realizing that Christ didn't want me to be with Him caused me more pain than knowing that I was going to hell. My greatest desire was to embrace Christ once before departing, but I knew that could never be. The entire judgment scene was instantaneous, but didn't seem rushed. In that instant, I didn't have to think about anything. There was no reasoning or arguing I just knew things, and knew my punishment was just.

Thankfully, I awoke before I journeyed to hell, but was left devastated nonetheless. Having the Being who I loved more than anyone turn me out of His presence was a horrifying experience. I sat in bed, wondering if that was the actual state of my soul. With more time to think, I realized that Christ didn't desire the separation, nor did He cause it. I had caused it with my sinfulness. Even in my dream, my self-centeredness was causing me to project the choice onto

Christ, instead of owning the responsibility myself. I had chosen my permanent separation from God by choosing sin.

The dream was wonderfully merciful though, and through it I received two primary gifts. The first was an improved understanding of my love for God. When everything else was stripped away, all I wanted was to throw myself into Christ and His all-encompassing love, light, and warmth. Only existence with God or without God was left. There was no more waiting in the arena to decide which path I wanted to choose. For years, my spiritual life was motivated primarily by a servile fear of an eternity in hell. I didn't openly want to offend God, but that wasn't my chief concern because I didn't know Him intimately. I went to weekly Mass and prayed when I thought about it, but I didn't really know Him. After what seemed to me as endless prayers petitioning God for the zeal necessary to pursue knowledge of Him, I finally started picking up pamphlets and books, and was drawn to websites that would aid me in my journey. In my mind, the whole process was too slow and I had to remind myself that God's timeline was not my timeline and to defer to His judgment. My love for God, while still vastly imperfect, was finally greater than my fear of hell, and this dream helped strengthen that conviction.

The second spiritual gift was a rededicated will to ensure that when my time of judgment comes, there will be no question about where my final resting place will be. I will continually try to maintain my focus on God, instead of on me. When I fail, I will return to Him to renew my spirit and begin again. In the end, this seemingly hopeless dream offered hope because I had not yet died, and the love of Christ was so real to me that it made me tremble.

None of that means my salvation is now assured or that I am holier than other people. Instead, I recognize that I am a work in progress who, through the grace of God, stopped rationalizing away responsibility for my actions. Rather than returning to Him for reconciliation once per year,

I now return regularly. God's love transformed my heart and I accepted that love.

The last chapter forewarned about parishes that teach only about love without broader formation or instruction. St. Clement of Alexandria wrote: "the first saving change is from paganism to faith, as I said before; and the second is that from faith to knowledge. This latter develops into love."[1] The formula outlined in the first chapter is know, love, and serve in that general order, and St. Clement recognized and taught that knowledge develops into love. Even though love generally follows knowledge, the importance of love is rooted in God's very nature, and its significance cannot be overstated. St. John told us that "God is love"[2] and the *Catechism of the Catholic Church* expounded on that by stating, "and love is the first gift, containing all others."[3]

Love is so important that when asked which was the greatest commandment, Christ Himself answered, "You shall love the Lord your God with all your heart, and with all your soul, and with all your mind. This is the great and first commandment. And a second is like it, You shall love your neighbor as yourself. On these two commandments depend all the law and the prophets."[4] Through love salvation is offered to us, and through love we are able to accept it. Everything proceeds from love.

Christ doesn't simply command us to love God, but in what might seem to be a radical stipulation, He called us to love others to the same degree that we love ourselves. That call was radical when Christ spoke those words, but it was not new. God gave the same law to Moses in the Old Testament some 1,500 years before Christ when He said, "you shall love your neighbor as yourself."[5] Love was central to God's plan for us from our beginning. God didn't create us out of need. We cannot (nor can any creature) add anything to God's holiness or wholeness. God is infinite and self-sufficient. He didn't create the human race or any individual human out of need; He created us out of love. God's gift of love is perfect, precisely because He shares it willingly, even though we cannot do or produce anything to enhance God's Being at any time now or in the future. God is love and desires that we share in His love.

At a weekend Mass, my pastor proposed in a recent homily that our greatest challenge is to let God love us. If we reflect on this suggestion, we will realize that God is obviously going to love us and doesn't need our permission to do so. How we respond to that love is the challenge. Will we accept God's love and let it transform and heal us, or will we turn from it and allow our spiritual growth to remain stagnant? The human soul is eternal and longs for love eternally. A soul can never be fully satiated by the objects of this world because they are finite and cannot fill an infinite need. Only God can fully satisfy the yearning in our soul, and He loves you more than you can know. No matter who you are and no matter what you have done, God loves you. His love is not conditional and not given to you because you've earned it. Your part is to accept that love and draw near to Him.

Until we understand God's love for us, we cannot recognize how we are called to love other people. His love is freely given, even when it is not sought. God's love is the most powerful force that exists because God is the most powerful force that exists. Love is eternal because God is eternal. God's love doesn't wax and wane; it is fully constant. When we feel it pull away, God's love does not weaken, but our connection to Him does. The change is on our end and not His. If we could only remember His love and never lose hope, then we would feel true joy in our hearts that would radiate out to the world. We would be in love with Him and for Him with His creation in this world.

From a human point of view, envisioning a love so complete and unwavering as the love of God is sometimes difficult. Much of our culture centers on a quid pro quo transactional approach to life. Connections are often, but not always, made with the expectation that we may need something at some point in the future. That something could be a sale, a favor, or preferential treatment for our children or for us. Such an expectation is not always ill-intended, and networking can be mutually beneficial. But God's love is different. We can please or displease Him, but nothing we do can add to nor subtract from His essence, because He is unchanging and unchangeable.

I once told a priest in confession that sometimes I had trouble believing that God would continually forgive the same sins no matter how many times I committed them. This kind father told me believing is not easy because we can't help but think of God in human terms. Most of us who were fortunate to have a loving mother knew we could continually fail her, and she would endlessly welcome us back. Mothers love us from the onset and we approach them for comfort and acceptance. He contrasted that with the experience many of us had with our fathers. Fathers are generally less effusive with praise, and we sometimes feel as though they withhold their approval until we earn it. They love us, but their love doesn't always appear to be unearned and freely given. As we call God "our Father," we have a tendency to view His love more in human terms and imagine that we have to earn it. In human terms, however, He loves us more like a mother.

What a beautiful means to better comprehend God's love for us. We can use the parent analogy in another way. God's love is personal, like that of an earthly parent. Consider these words from Christ: "Are not five sparrows sold for two pennies? And not one of them is forgotten before God. Why, even the hairs of your head are all numbered. Fear not; you are of more value than many sparrows."[6] He is conscious about even the hairs on our heads. God, the creator of everything, doesn't just love us in a general way like we might love animals or a group of animals like dolphins. He knows us and loves us specifically as individuals. In the Book Of Jeremiah, God affirmed, "Before I formed you in the womb I knew you."[7] He has always loved us individually. As my own children were born, I became convinced that God had blessed me with them so I could begin to understand how much He loves me. The intensity isn't the same, though. No matter what love I muster for my children, it is incomparably inferior to the love God has for my children and me.

The analogy is still useful and any parent can take it one step further. Most parents' greatest desire is for their children to love, support, and care for each other, much in the same way God desires that for all of His children. A parent might ask with exasperation "Can't you just be kind to each other?" or "Can you please stop fighting?" When an earthly parent asks such questions, it seems, at least to the parent, that the child should be able to comply easily. What about when our heavenly parent asks the same question of us? What seemed to be a simple question when we asked it of our children doesn't seem to scale as well when posed to us.

Christ requires us to love as mentioned above and throughout Scripture. He doesn't leave us wondering as to what love obliges on our part. Christ very directly said, "If you love me, you will keep my commandments."[8] That simple text doesn't leave a lot of wiggle room for rationalization. After reading that Scripture, saying "Well, I definitely love God and certainly keep the big commandments like murder, and well, most of the others most of the time" is much more difficult. The inescapable truth is that God is love and sin can never abide in God, so sin is never love.

Love isn't some soft idea that doesn't require us to do anything other than feel. Love is an action verb, just like those we learned about in our early school years. To love can be hard. When you love someone, you do what's in his or her best interest, even when it is not convenient or comfortable for you. The degree to which you love them will dictate how much you will sacrifice.

Sacrifice doesn't always relate to time, money, or material goods. In some cases, sacrifice means enduring spiritual or emotional pain. One Catholic dictionary defines love of neighbor as desiring the true good (eternal life) of others.[9] Desiring salvation for others is the only permanent and lasting love. Rightly ordered love never works against the salvation of an individual for any reason. Open-mindedness has regrettably become synonymous with rejecting the concept of absolute truth, and professing that all opinions are equally true and valid. Since Christ is absolute truth, you must reject that definition or you will reject Him. Instead, consider yourself openhearted and love all people regardless of their current state because we are all sinners. Christ sat not with the saints but with the sinners, and He loved them all. Don't exclude or ostracize anyone, but remember always that the first order of loving your neighbor is to care for his or her eternal salvation. Never lead others to believe sin is not sin, or that sin is acceptable to God. Doing so risks you being partially culpable for the loss of another soul. It also endangers your own soul; as we read in the Book of Isaiah: "Woe to those who call evil good and good evil."[10] Proverbs makes a similar point: "He who winks the eye causes trouble, but he who boldly reproves makes peace."[11] Everyone has a right to their own opinion through God's gift of free will, but they are not all equally true.

Standing with Christ in our society isn't universally popular, and doing so will most likely cause you suffering. Many people have ceased being able to recognize the definition of love as it was given to humans through the Bible. St. Paul gave us one of the most compelling, beautiful, and true depictions of love:

> "Love is patient and kind; love is not jealous or boastful; it is not arrogant or rude. Love does not insist on its own way; it is not irritable or resentful; it does not rejoice at wrong, but rejoices in the right. Love bears all things, believes all things, hopes all things, endures all things. Love never ends."[12]

Notice that among other points, St. Paul conveys the frequently ignored concept that love does not rejoice in wrong. We hear this reading most often at weddings, and tend to focus on what we may consider the nice parts of love, such as patience and kindness. But we must embrace the entire definition. Frequently, people will seek either your tacit or explicit approval for their sinful behavior. Whether this situation occurs at school, the office, in social settings, or the like-out of love, make your primary concern the eternal well-being of the parties involved. Resist the urge to approve of or participate in anything that you know is contrary to God's will.

That doesn't mean that you must actively begin confronting everyone who you suspect might be engaged in sin. In fact, Christ cautioned against that when He said: "Why do you see the speck that is in your brother's eye, but do not notice the log that is in your own eye?"[13] We should never rejoice in wrong but also never dare to tell an individual or group that they are going to hell. Nor should we stand idly by while society deteriorates or an individual continues on a self-destructive path. One of the corporal works of mercy is to admonish the sinner. Love people and draw them toward what is beautiful through that love. Look for opportunities to share without confrontation and without accusation. Pray for them. We can't judge another person's soul, but we can educate and encourage them to seek God's will in their lives and grow in their faith by pursuing knowledge through His church on Earth. On a societal level, we certainly can and should stand against evils like abortion, euthanasia, and pornography.

When you do stand for God and against evil, you will be attacked and hated. St. Faustina told us: "The quintessence of love is sacrifice and suffering. Truth wears a crown of thorns."[14] But Christ comforted us with the words: "If the world hates you, know that it has hated me before it hated you. If you were of the world, the world would love its own;

but because you are not of the world, but I chose you out of the world, therefore the world hates you."[15] What they may really hate is the feeling in their conscience when they must confront their own rejection of God, who is love. St. Augustine put this sentiment another way: "Therefore they hate the truth for the sake of whatever it is that they love in place of the truth. They love truth when she shines on them; and hate her when she rebukes them."[16]

St. Paul referred to many other properties of love and these too must be equally honored. When you find yourself being particularly patient, recognize that quality as love and be mindful of your closeness to God. Such an acknowledgment will strengthen your bond with Him and increase the virtue of patience within you. Conversely, if you find yourself harboring feelings of jealousy or resentfulness, be aware that those feelings are not love, and ask God to help refocus your thoughts toward a more loving orientation. Be present in the moment when particular trials test a willingness to endure all things, and see endurance as an act of love. The more often you can recognize love in the present moment, the easier choosing it becomes in the next.

When considering St. Paul's definition, understand that being kind and being nice are different. Being nice is important, but isn't always good. Nice people are generally agreeable, but not always in an honest way. Niceness is a reactive and passive state of being. Being kind is an active state of expressing God's love by doing something out of concern for your neighbor. Kindness is opening a door or carrying in the groceries without being asked. It's a spiritual or corporal act of mercy, in which there is an action, not a reaction. To be kind is to be considerate of another person's feelings with sincerity and truthfulness. Kindness is being empathetic and working on that empathy in a spirit of truth. Unlike being nice, kindness can never be faked because it is always an action done out of love. That's not to say being nice is always or even mostly fake or insincere, but it can be.

Niceness can be superficial depending on its source, but kindness's one face is the face of love.

Notice, too, that St. Paul's definition of love does not include pleasure as one of love's attributes. Love and pleasure are two different concepts. In today's vernacular, love and pleasure, or enjoyment, are often used interchangeably. The lack of precision in word choice and thinking often leads to confusion in moral choices. This confusion unfortunately, is exacerbated by maxims such as "If it feels good then do it." Exclaiming that you love chocolate ice cream because you really enjoy it is not sinful. Recognize, though, the biblical meaning of love, and understand that ice cream is not God, so it's not really love. Sexual intercourse is the most obvious example of pleasure posing as love. Often, it has been given the misnomer of "making love." God is love and God is not made, so love is not made. Love instead is expressed and sexual relations, inside of a sacramental marriage, are an expression of love and self-giving. Sharing a bowl of ice cream can also be an expression of love and self-giving. Both are examples of God's loving gifts to us as we were created with the ability to enjoy corporal pleasure. Rightly ordered pleasure contains no shame or sin. Pleasure outside of God's intent, however, is outside of His will and is sin, and therefore, not love.

Perhaps the best synonym for love is selflessness. St. Paul's definition and other examples in Scripture essentially direct us toward the needs of others. Loving yourself is not wrong, and desiring salvation for yourself should be your primary concern. When you love yourself, though, don't love yourself for who you are, but because God made you and your love will never be disordered. Selflessness may be the single most difficult struggle against our nature.

To become selfless we must see others as God sees them. One conduit to that vision is picturing how God sees and loves us with all our faults and projecting that approach to others. In doing so, recall God's personal love and attentiveness. When Christ tells us to love our enemies,[17] He's not exclusively referring to some foreign army halfway across the globe bent on our destruction. Love is much more personal than that. His instruction is about the people in your everyday life who maintain real or imagined animosity toward you. Our call as Christians is to respond with the love of kindness and prayer. The Apostle John taught: "If any one says, "I love God," and hates his brother, he is a liar; for he who does not love his brother whom he has seen, cannot love God whom he has not seen."[18] Love heals and drives out hate. It may not heal the relationship, but love will heal the person who feels the scorn of another.

Personal love isn't just for friends and enemies; people whom we are called to love surround us. Christ told the story of a rich man and a poor man named Lazarus.[19] The rich man lived a comfortable life with all of his needs met. Lazarus lived outside the rich man's door in total poverty. Both died; Lazarus rests in peace and the rich man resides in hell for his lack of love toward Lazarus. The rich man had every opportunity and more than enough prosperity to lift Lazarus up while on Earth, but never did. When this Scripture was read at Mass, the priest asked us to consider two questions as we left. Who are the invisible people in your life who need you to love them? Who is your Lazarus? That homily had a strong impact on me, and I have never stopped thinking about it.

The opportunity to love in a very personal way is before us all, and like the rich man, we don't need to search far to find it. Love can be expressed with a kind word or a greeting to a stranger as you pass on the street. It can be found in the company of a relative or friend who aches for companionship. Love can manifest itself in a commitment to chastity, desiring salvation more for your partner than desiring pleasure for yourself. Love is listening to an unreasonable friend who has no one else who will listen. It is attending the function you'd rather not attend, knowing how much your presence means to the host. Volunteering at your church or local charitable organization, or donating your treasure to a worthy cause shows a strong commitment to love. Sharing your faith is a meritorious act of love. Christ gave us the sacraments of the church, particularly the Holy Eucharist, to express His love to us. When we participate in the sacraments, we accept and bear witness to others of His great love for us.

Love can be expressed in a myriad of ways too numerous to list. Acts of mercy, in particular, epitomize love in a unique and extraordinary way. Even the word "mercy" is beautiful to our ears. Mercy proceeds from love and is often misunderstood or misapplied. The next chapter will examine God's mercy toward us and reveal the key to accepting it.

Chapter 6: Mercy

Mercy seems like such a benign word, but it has become a lightning rod in various Catholic circles. The concept of mercy rankles the sensibilities of some who believe God's goodness is being abused as justification for all manner of sinfulness. They are embittered to realize that while they lived in faithfulness, others lived in sin and still claimed the same treasure at the last minute. They question the veracity of (and doubt the sincerity of) the recently repentant, putting them in the perilous position of judging another's soul.

This conflict is as old as the Bible. Recall from chapter four the elder son in the story of the prodigal son. Having mercy extended from the father to his wayward brother offended his sense of fairness. Christ told another parable that likens the kingdom of heaven to laborers in a vineyard.[1] A landowner hired laborers throughout the day to work in his vineyard. At the end of the day, he paid each laborer the same wage, irrespective of the number of hours worked. The laborers who toiled the entire day were resentful when they realized they received the same compensation as those who worked only an hour. Both the father in the first parable and the landowner in the second make clear that mercy extended to latecomers does not diminish the reward to the long-term faithful.

In the opposite faction are those who wield the word "mercy" against the faithful as though it were a weapon. They mistakenly believe that God's mercy is synonymous with God's acceptance of sin. Presumption of God's mercy is a great sin. *The Catholic Encyclopedia* defined it as "the condition of a soul which, because of a badly regulated reliance on God's mercy and power, hopes for salvation without doing anything to deserve it, or for pardon of his sins without repenting of them."[2] Grouped in a loose confederation with these presumptuous souls are those relying on a last-minute repentance to secure their salvation. Mercy is their backup plan if they run out of time. The approach is ill-conceived as God told us through St. Catherine: "although every one may and should hope as long as he has life, he should not put such trust in this hope as to delay repentance."[3]

The fundamental misunderstanding of mercy has been exacerbated by press coverage, particularly in the Holy Year of Mercy. Mercy is presented as some type of magical "get out of jail free" card. Everyone has one and they need only show their pass to God to gain admission to heaven. Even before the Holy Year of Mercy, Pope Francis continually had his words misquoted, taken out of context, or both. The UK based Independent ran a headline on September 11, 2013, that reported "Pope Francis assures atheists: You don't have to believe in God to go to heaven."[4] The Internet and blogosphere exploded with similar headlines. If you read the stories, you would learn that is not, in fact, what the Pope said. Pope Francis said: "The Lord has redeemed all of us, all of us, with the Blood of Christ: all of us, not just Catholics. Everyone! 'Father, the atheists?' Even the atheists. Everyone! And this Blood makes us children of God."[5] He further went on to suggest that if we all do good works, we could meet in the midst of those good works.

A layperson or nonbeliever may not understand the difference between redemption and salvation or that all people are children of God, whether they acknowledge Him or not. Pope Francis's accessibility has led to this and other mischaracterizations of his teachings. Ignorance creates confusion where there should be none, and the press is eager to disseminate diluted or false Catholic teaching. Attributing distortions to the leader of the faith further wounds in two ways. The misrepresentation can neutralize the call to conversion for those living outside the will of God. Why would anyone seek God, if even the Pope were actually to believe that living a generally good life and performing good deeds was enough to accept salvation? Second, these diabolic attacks create division within the church and turn faithful Catholics against the Pontiff and against one another. The stories are designed to generate doubt in the minds of the faithful.

Whether people are anticipating changes in church teaching in hope or in angst, they will discover that those changes are not coming. Rituals and ceremonial law may change, but doctrinal teachings never will. They are from God, who is unchanging and unchangeable. Expect the secular media to continue misrepresentations, but dig deeper into stories and use authentic Catholic sources to enhance your understanding and knowledge.

The definition of mercy, likewise, is not changing. Mercy is not a panacea or free pass for unrepentant sinfulness and the rejection of God's call in a soul. Indeed, it doesn't exist in such cases. According to the *Compendium of the Catechism of the Catholic Church*, "It requires that we admit our faults and repent of our sins."[6] Repentance is the key to the acceptance of God's mercy. This requirement is not negotiable, not acceptable in half-measures, and not merely a suggestion; it's absolute. Christ extended mercy to the woman caught in adultery. After He saved her from stoning, His parting words were "go, and do not sin again."[7] Christ's call to repentance is not a call to perfection, but rather a call to strive daily toward perfection. Mercy is a sharing of His grace to help us stay on the right path and strengthen us against falling back into sin. Some people recognized as saints perfectly ceded their will to God, and reached full purification on Earth. The rest of us must resolve to continue trying, and reconciling with God when we fall short.

God's mercy cannot be earned; it must be accepted. Forgiveness is always available for us through God's infinite well of mercy, but we must seek it through repentance. From 1 John: "If we confess our sins, he is faithful and just, and will forgive our sins and cleanse us from all unrighteousness."[8] Mercy and justice are inextricably intertwined. Christ told St. Faustina in a vision: "before I come as a just Judge, I first open wide the door of My mercy. He who refuses to pass through the door of My mercy must pass through the door of My justice."[9] If we make an informed evaluation of these alternatives, mercy seems the obvious choice. It costs something in this temporary life, but justice would cost everything in the next permanent life. We can choose mercy, which we don't deserve but is still available to us, or we can choose justice and the consequences thereof.

Mercy proceeds from love and therefore is not sin. When evil masquerades as mercy, there seems to be no limit to the depth of depravity reached. Abortion was positioned as an act of mercy for children who would be born into difficult economic or health circumstances. Margaret Sanger, the founder of Planned Parenthood wrote, "The most merciful thing that the large family does to one of its infant members is to kill it."[10] Abortionists hide behind a false notion of mercy toward women, while they line their pockets with money made from human sacrifice. That act is not mercy; it is sin. Depriving a child of his or her life, regardless of the circumstances, is not an act of love.

On the other hand, true mercy from God cannot be confined or contained. Pope Francis wrote, "Mercy will always be greater than any sin, and no one can place limits on the love of God who is ever ready to forgive."[11] Christ appeared in a vision to St. Faustina and referred to Himself as the Divine Mercy. He told her: "Let the weak, sinful soul have no fear to approach Me, for even if it had more sins than there are grains of sand in the world, all would be drowned in the unmeasurable depths of My mercy."[12]

When Christ spoke of the "weak, sinful soul," He was speaking to each of us, especially those who are far from Him. In the Gospel According to St. Luke, Christ made the point that those who have been forgiven much will love much, and those who have been forgiven little will love little.[13] Recall also Christ's words as He hung on the cross:

"Father, forgive them; for they know not what they do."[14] What guilt could possibly surpass the torture and execution of Christ and yet, He forgave them. Even to consider such depth of mercy is astonishing.

In another remarkable expression of God's mercy, He shared the following with St. Catherine: "My mercy is greater without any comparison than all the sins which any creature can commit; wherefore it greatly displeases Me that they should consider their sins to be greater."[15] Hearing people say, even in a half-joking manner, that they are too far gone to come back to God is heartbreaking. That conviction is never true, but people often fall into despair. God addressed this topic to St. Catherine as well, telling her that the sin of despair displeases Him more and damages the soul more than all the other sins that they have committed.[16] Despair is Satan's vice grip that holds sinners in a place where they feel they can no longer reach God. That is never true either; there is always hope. God can reach willing souls in any place they find themselves. Despondent souls no longer hope for their own salvation. Despair, like presumption, precludes repentance, thereby rejecting God's mercy and forgiveness. If this unwillingness to repent becomes a permanent state, it leads to eternal loss and damnation. Pray particularly for despondent souls and fear your own propensity to sin, but trust in God's mercy to give you the graces to avoid sins that lead to final death. From Hebrews: "Let us then with confidence draw near to the throne of grace, that we may receive mercy and find grace to help in time of need."[17]

Many people tend to associate the greatness of God's mercy more with the New Testament than with the Old Testament. Like love, however, mercy was present from the beginning. In Exodus, we read: "The Lord passed before him, and proclaimed, "The Lord, the Lord, a God merciful and gracious, slow to anger, and abounding in steadfast love and faithfulness.""[18] One of the most well-known Psalms expresses the breadth of God's mercy "as far as the east is from the west, so far does he remove our transgressions from us."[19] Among numerous other references to mercy in the Old Testament are the stories of two cities. Sodom, in the Book of Genesis and Nineveh, in the book of Jonah, were both brimming with sinfulness. God was willing to save Sodom for the sake of just ten righteous people, but found only four. Still, He offered repentance through obedience to those four people and led them out of the city before it was destroyed. Jonah visited Nineveh and called the people to repent. They did and the city was spared. These two examples of God extending mercy, one accepted and one rejected, offer a parallel to God's call to accept His mercy in our lives.

Accepting mercy in our lives is much broader than simply accepting reconciliation with God. Mercy is an approach to life and the implementation of love. Mercy is one of the fruits of love.[20] It grows from the tree of love and just as you know an apple tree by its fruit, you will recognize a loving person through his or her acts of mercy. If love were an operating system, mercy would be one of its applications. Just as God required us to extend His love to others, He also obliged us to deal mercifully with them when He told us, "Be merciful, even as your Father is merciful."[21] When Peter asked Christ how many times he must forgive his neighbor, Christ told him seventy-seven times which is to say, an unlimited number of times. [22]

The link between how we treat others and how God has treated us is a recurrent theme throughout the Bible. In the Beatitudes, Christ said very simply: "Blessed are the merciful, for they shall obtain mercy."[23] The connection is expressed, perhaps even more powerfully, when Christ said, "Truly, I say to you, as you did it to one of the least of these my brethren, you did it to me."[24] In this last verse particularly, we can grasp that the reason we must treat our neighbor mercifully is for the love of God. Christ's brothers are God's children, and a display of mercy toward them is a display of love toward God, who is love. St. Faustina wrote in her diary, "We resemble God most when we forgive our neighbors."[25]

As with love, we must extend mercy personally to others. Mercy isn't an abstract idea to be considered from afar. Perhaps the most rewarding manifestation of God's love, mercy connects us to others and through them to God. In our lives, mercy should be considerably more extensive than solely forgiveness. The church provides a list of works of mercy to better enable us to envision and perform personal acts of mercy. They are separated into two groups: one for the physical well-being of a person, and one for the spiritual well-being of the soul.

The Seven Corporal Works of Mercy[26]

- Feed the hungry
- Give drink to the thirsty
- Clothe the naked
- Shelter the homeless
- Visit the sick
- Visit the imprisoned
- Bury the dead

The Seven Spiritual Works of Mercy

- Counsel the doubtful
- Instruct the ignorant
- Admonish sinners
- Comfort the afflicted
- Forgive offenses
- Bear wrongs patiently
- Pray for the living and the dead

These acts of mercy bring healing to a world that is hurting. Sr. Marie Veritas of the Sisters of Life in New York recently wrote, "Mercy draws good from evil. It is the love that does not allow itself to be conquered by evil, pain, or suffering, but overcomes evil with good."[27] What a wonderful way to portray mercy. Mercy is the salve on the wounds of the world. It's a powerful elixir of love, whose healing properties touch both body and soul. As we bring mercy into the world, we bring witness of Christ's love and evangelize in a way that words can never match. We have considerably more wealth and plenty of freedom compared to our ancestors, and we choose to spend so much of both on sin. Imagine how much good there would be in the world if we turned our resources away from vice and toward virtue through acts of mercy. Consider choosing at least one of these acts to perform each day, and let them transform not only the recipient, but also the benefactor.

Many books and blogs are available to explore each of these works in more depth. The corporal works seem more straightforward, but even they deserve thoughtful meditation. And aside from these works make a commitment to walk in mercy. Each day, we have the opportunity to reflect God's loving mercy in the way we react to events and people around us. When the shaming story of the day appears in the news, pray for the person who made the mistake, and thank God that person wasn't you. When a topic comes up online, avoid the urge to respond in kind to the ugly and hateful comments directed at your position or perhaps even at you. Never allow yourself to state that there is a special place in hell for a particular person because of something he or she did. The more you walk in mercy, the more you will recoil at those types of behaviors. That is how you will know you are on the right track. Approach sinners especially with love and mercy. You cannot save them. Christ will do that if they accept Him, but you can love them and show them by your actions that there is a way that is better than all of these.

Finally, hold yourself accountable for always trying to do better but when you fall short, acknowledge the failing, accept it, and move on. We all make mistakes, hurt others, and have regrets, but valuing yourself based on mistakes you've made is an unfair standard for anyone. Christian musician Ricardo Sanchez once said: "The devil knows your name but calls you by your sin. God knows your sin but calls you by your name."[28] Apply the adage "love the sinner but hate the sin" to yourself, and detest your sin without falling into the trap of self-loathing. We are not defined by our sin. Doing so impersonalizes us, rejecting the dignity of our humanity. People dehumanizing their opponents, so they can treat them with contempt without feeling the same pang of conscience that they should, has been a regular pattern throughout history. That degradation comes not from God, but from Satan. Don't believe it about yourself or others.

Salvation, love, and mercy are all gifts bestowed on a soul who draws near to God. Unfortunately, not everything we can expect to experience will be as pleasant. Some things are more difficult to understand and more difficult to bear. The next chapter examines our walk with God in a way and to a place that none prefer to go.

Chapter 7: Suffering

On a December evening that began like any other, my family finished dinner and departed to complete our remaining tasks for the day. The date was less than a week before Christmas and one of my sisters wanted to go to the store to pick up a few things. She asked me to ride along and I was happy to oblige. The night seems eons ago in a technological sense (no cell phones, no PCs, etc.), but like yesterday in every other. As I said good-bye to my dad, he was having indigestion that we all figured was his gallbladder acting up again. I hugged him and he reassured me that it'd be all right. A different sister offered to take him to the hospital to get checked out, so off we went to the store and off they went to the hospital.

On our way home, without a care in the world, my sister and I neared the turn for our street and were both suddenly overcome with a foreboding sense that something was terribly wrong. When we entered the house, one of my brothers was staring through the picture window. Slowly, he turned and said, "Dad died tonight." Already on edge, I rebuked him and told him that wasn't funny. He lowered his head and told me it wasn't a joke; it had really happened. I fell to my knees in agony, my heart collapsing in upon itself. Whatever I thought I knew about grief, I didn't know. Prior suffering was nothing compared to the anguish that I began experiencing in that moment. I wanted the earth to open and swallow me, but there was no escape. I cried until I was numb.

My innocence died forever after that car ride home, and I have never been the same. I have often rued my naive sense of security. Hugging my father while he was having a massive heart attack and not recognizing the signs. Not realizing that was our last embrace or spending his last minutes on Earth with him haunted me for years. Foolishly believing he was just having indigestion, and not even considering for a second that anything worse could happen. My pain was my own, and although I knew my siblings and mother were suffering in the same way, I never spoke of it to them or to anyone else. The world had become a different place. I seemed to be walking through a detached plane of reality as I drifted past people whose lives had remained unchanged. How could they go on as though nothing had happened when inside I knew everything was different? When I returned to school, none of the kids could look at me and the teachers glanced at me with such sorrow. One of my friends mentioned that they'd discussed my father's sudden death in class before I returned, but said no more. Braver souls told me that if I needed someone to talk to, they were there for me, but they didn't understand; I didn't know how to talk about it. My dad understood me so well, and now he was gone forever. My isolation was suffocating. He was a good man; why did such a terrible thing have to happen to him, to us, to me?

Suffering, like love and like mercy, is intensely personal. The topic is such a difficult one to discuss. We all want desperately to help other people avoid suffering, but we know that there is no escaping; they or we must go through it. Suffering is hard for most of us to grasp. It seems a distasteful and meaningless element of our existence. Understanding why suffering is necessary is tough. I'd like this chapter to be the shortest in the book, as I'd like the experience of suffering to be the shortest chapter in our lives. Unfortunately, life doesn't always work that way.

In my adult years, I have attended wakes for different friends' fathers. On more than one occasion, I have had the bereaved tell me that they know their suffering isn't like what I went through. There's a social expectation that we should grieve less for elderly relatives who pass away because they lived a full life. But my loss and my suffering don't diminish anyone else's mourning because it is personal to them.

Empathy is possible when we accept that one type of suffering does not trump another. And we can use it to connect with those who are suffering if it manifests in simply being present and loving toward them.

Suffering takes many forms. Losing something dear to us, whether it is a job, a relationship, or a loved one causes pain. Loss is the sort of suffering that we try to recover from, but there are others we have to learn to endure. Chronic illness, social isolation, poverty, self-doubt, depression, hunger, imprisonment, persecution, and seeing loved ones turn away from God are just a sampling of suffering that require endurance. All are real, and all are personal.

Suffering is also universal. St. Augustine expressed this attribute of suffering well when he said, "God had one Son on earth without sin, but never one without suffering."[1] We have all either suffered, or know of people who have suffered greatly and may continue to suffer. If you read about the saints, you will find most of their lives were full of both spiritual and physical suffering. When they weren't suffering a physical malady, they willingly sacrificed comfort in order to make reparations to God for their sins or for the sins of the world. Many, like St. Faustina, expressed to God the willingness and desire to suffer and subsequently, did suffer greatly. Other saints received the stigmata, the wounds of Christ. Catholics hold such saints in high regard and think how wonderfully holy they were to receive such a blessing. The physical pain and embarrassment of these saints is often forgotten. So, too, are the sacrifices made by the saints to put them in state of grace wherein the stigmata became possible. Many saints have been tortured and martyred for the faith, suffering terrible deaths. Christ Himself suffered for all of us, and His sacrifice didn't begin with His passion. His earthly life was one of prayer and fasting.

Suffering is real, personal, universal, and also necessary. It is part of God's plan. In a vision, God told St. Catherine, "Because you cannot pass this mortal life without pain, and in Me, the Father, there can be no pain, but in Him (the son) there can be pain, and therefore of Him did I make for you a Bridge."[2] Most of us would prefer to approach the Father directly without suffering. Had sin not entered the world that path would have been possible, but it is no longer so. Even Mary, who was born without original sin and who remained sinless throughout her life, suffered greatly while on Earth.

At a memorial Mass for my father, the priest spoke in his homily of Christ's suffering on the cross. The world was in a downward spiral, and with Roman soldiers torturing and killing Christ, evil seemed to be winning the day. The priest pointed out that even in that darkest hour, God was still in control. Those who witnessed the crucifixion didn't understand the event at the time, but it was all part of God's plan. God was using the soldiers and the suffering of Christ for His end. The soldiers were playing right into God's hands. We know in the end that the goodness and power of God will triumph over evil. Like the apostles, we may not recognize or even like the plan; however, there is a context that makes suffering more meaningful and removes its air of fruitlessness. As unpleasant as suffering is, it serves a purpose.

A fair amount of praying is oriented toward petitioning God to free us from or help us avoid suffering and pain. God desires us to draw near to Him, and the presence of suffering drives us to do just that. Most people have heard the familiar old saying that there's no atheist in a foxhole. Absolutes when describing people don't usually stand up, but I can tell you that the general sentiment is true. Fortunately, when I served in the Army National Guard, I never had to go to war, but basic training was an eight-week sufferfest. Lying in my bunk at night, I'd listen to guys crying because they were homesick, in pain, feeling defeated, empty, desperate, and afraid. We'd wish the night wouldn't end so we wouldn't have to face the drill sergeants and the misery they brought in the morning. Even then, I knew guys would go home and tell people how the experience was nothing and they had no problems at all. Know, though, that no one was happy. It was like being in prison. If you have ever been really heartbroken, you know that a lump in your throat is a real thing, a physical manifestation of grief. Homesickness is also a physical manifestation of loss, and you really do feel sick. We were a platoon of miserable, weary, young men who'd made a choice that we couldn't rescind, and we had nothing left except God. Virtually everyone went to church, and Sunday was the best day of the week. I now realize what a short period of time basic training was, but at that time and age, it was tough for everyone.

When we moved on, advanced individual training was still challenging but not in the same way. Sadly, many left their thirst for God behind in basic training. Drawing near to God in times of trouble and wandering away from Him in times of plenty is part of a pattern. That ebb and flow is not part of God's plan, but a failure on our part to remain unwaveringly committed to Him. That approach squanders the hard-won opportunity to have forged a closer communion with God and essentially, undoes the progress achieved. Souls who recognize the pattern are the most likely ones to avoid it.

In addition to drawing us nearer to God, suffering helps us better understand His infinite goodness. In loss there is emptiness, a need or desire that can no longer be fulfilled. Something finite has changed or departed. Indeed, nothing on Earth can provide us with infinite unchanging happiness because it is all finite and changeable. Understanding the finite nature of what was lost and our aching need for it should lead to gratitude toward God who alone can fulfill our infinite needs. When you experience loss, focus on the knowledge that when you rejoin God, you will never again feel that separation or pain. The taste of suffering increases the thirst for God. He gives us the separation now so that we desire Him all the more and work toward being with Him by living, as He would have us live. Suffering helps souls focus on the purpose of life. In what may seem counterintuitive, St. Paul spoke of suffering as a gift.[3] In this context, we begin to see that in some aspects, it is a gift.

St. Peter told us that God allows suffering to test us. "In this you rejoice, though now for a little while you may have to suffer various trials, so that the genuineness of your faith, more precious than gold which though perishable is tested by fire, may redound to praise and glory and honor at the revelation of Jesus Christ."[4] St. Padre Pio expounded on this sentiment when he wrote: "The more you are afflicted, the more you ought to rejoice, because in the fire of tribulation the soul will become pure gold, worthy to be placed and to shine in the heavenly palace."[5] Loving and being thankful to God for His goodness is easy when life seems to be going well. When we are suffering, do we still love God through our pain? Do we still desire and love Him above all else? Suffering presents the occasion to demonstrate faithfulness to God through our response to it. We will still feel sadness, and in fact, St. Paul shared an example of sorrow for the loss of a loved one that does not offend God.[6] The appropriate response to sorrow is turning toward and not away from God. How we answer this test can be used as a guidepost for spiritual development. Free will makes the love in us real and suffering validates our choices, thereby increasing self-knowledge. Self-knowledge can be used to adjust and renew a commitment to God.

Suffering also purifies us. Christ died to redeem us, opening the path to heaven, and through baptism, original sin was removed and the fullness of God's grace renewed. In the sacrament of reconciliation, we receive absolution for our sins of omission or commission, but still must make atonement for the temporal punishment attached to those transgressions. Atonement can be accomplished through prayer, almsgiving, charitable works, and suffering. We can also offer suffering for the atonement of others. St. Paul pointed out that we could be heirs with Christ if we suffer with Him.[7] Suffering further purifies by increasing virtue, moving us closer to the perfect love of Christ.

Growing up, my mother often told me to offer my suffering up for the souls in purgatory. As a child, I had no idea what she was talking about. As a teenager, I'd openly question what the point of that was; I was going to suffer anyway. As an adult, I realized that *was* the point. We are going to suffer anyway, whether we are willing to offer our suffering up or not. How we accept the suffering in our lives constitutes our level of sacrifice. St. John Vianney, in a brilliant sermon on suffering, wrote specifically on suffering well versus suffering badly:

> "Whether we will or not, we must suffer. There are some who suffer like the good thief, and others who suffer like the bad thief. They both suffered alike, but the one made his sufferings meritorious-he accepted them in a spirit of reparation; and, turning towards Jesus crucified, he received from His lips these gracious words: "Today shalt thou be with me in Paradise." The other, on the contrary, continued to vociferate imprecations and blasphemies, and expired in frightful despair. There are two ways of suffering: to suffer with love, and to suffer without love." [8]

How we accept suffering correlates to its level of merit. Our acceptance of God's will in our lives, even through suffering, brings us into closer communion with Him. When Christ returned to Nazareth, the people had heard of the wonders He had performed and wanted the same for themselves. They didn't receive the miracles they desired, so they responded with anger and tried to force the Lord out of their lives by throwing Him off a cliff.[9] Do we respond likewise when our suffering isn't relieved in the way we had hoped? When we must endure suffering or confront some terrible loss, do we turn Christ out of our lives? In this Scripture we can easily spot the wrongheadedness of such an approach. Sometimes in our own lives it is more difficult to see.

Life rarely turns out as we planned. When something bad happens to us, as humans, we often fall into the trap of asking if God really loves us. The correct question actually is: Do we really love God, even given the test through which we must pass? Some people are born into suffering and have a particularly difficult cross to bear in this life. For them, suffering can be a lifelong test and they similarly may ask if God really loves them. The answer is He does and He is present with us, even when we don't recognize Him.

On a hike through the woods, I often return by the same trail on which I departed. The second time through invariably brings me past something beautiful that I didn't notice on my first pass. Maybe it was a particular tree or the way a brook cascaded down a rock embankment. A lack of focus on it during my initial pass didn't mean that it wasn't there, but rather that I didn't make myself aware of it. God's presence in our suffering is sometimes like that. We think He wasn't there when, truthfully, we didn't see Him. When we look back with a clearer head and more focus, we might see Him in a neighbor or a friend who reached out to us. Perhaps He was there in a song or homily that seemed to speak directly to us. Sometimes God will keep us busy with work or other tasks to help us get through a difficult time. Maybe He was with us in a still, quiet moment when we were exhausted from grief and exhaled during a respite between sobs, His voice quieting our hearts, whispering His presence, comforting our souls. His plans are not always evident, but His love is never absent; it is personal and it is for you.

You can go through difficult periods by leaning on God or without leaning on God. In either case, the suffering will be the same, but the ease and merit with which you bear it will be diametrically opposed, both in the short and long term. We can look to the saints as examples of bravely accepting the will of God when it involved suffering or distress. One of my favorite stories is of St. Francisco Marto, who was one of the children who saw Our Lady at Fatima. In 1919, at just ten years of age, he was stricken with the Spanish flu, in what was sure to be a fatal infection. He welcomed the illness as a promise from Our Blessed Mother to take him to heaven.[10] This little boy faced his fate with the courage of a lion. Books on the saints are filled with similarly inspiring tales; take advantage of them. They will help in difficult times.

Even understanding some of the context of suffering and that the saints often welcomed it may not make it less painful. But I hope the perspective presented in this chapter will make suffering more meaningful and make it easier for you to connect with God as you move through it. The Book of Sirach contains this advice: "Accept whatever is brought upon you, and in changes that humble you be patient. For gold is tested in the fire, and acceptable men in the furnace of humiliation."[11]

Only through faith can we attain a holy acceptance of suffering. We explore the power of faith in the next chapter, looking at examples of great faith and learning about some surprising people who struggled with it from the start.

Part Three

How Should We Approach God?

In Him We Live and Move and Have Our Being
(Acts 17:28)

Chapter 8: Faith

When faith touches a soul, it can leave a lasting imprint. It kindles inside and bursts forth to shine in unexpected ways. My wife is a cantor in our local parish collaborative and often sings at funerals. After Mass one day, she introduced me to a couple who had recently lost their adult son. They shared some kind words about my wife's singing as I shook their hands in greeting. There was a certain resignation about them, and I prayed in my head not to say the wrong thing. I could see a tear welling in the woman's eye as she told me this was the second son they had lost. Looking past me, she then said, "That was God's will, I don't know why it was, but we have to accept it." Her beautiful faith shone like a bright light even through the darkest of trials. Like the apostles during Christ's passion and crucifixion, she didn't understand the plan. Even so, she wasn't avoiding people and mourning alone, but testifying to the truth. Her answer to the unimaginable suffering of losing two children was to put her faith and trust in God. Witnessing such great faith in light of so significant a loss was humbling. Faith, as one of the three theological virtues, is a gift from God, and He shared that gift of faith with and through this gentle woman.

Scripture defines faith as follows: "Now faith is the assurance of things hoped for, the conviction of things not seen. For by it the men of old received divine approval. By faith we understand that the world was created by the word of God, so that what is seen was made out of things which do not appear."[1]

Faith is the gift that draws us in and keeps us tethered to God. It is the acceptance and belief in God's word. Beyond simply belief, faith is a trust that God knows what is best and will furnish what we need for our salvation, even when we don't understand the plan. Perfect faith manifests itself in perfect trust. Christ told us to seek His kingdom and the Father will provide what we need.[2] We must accept this gift with simplicity and approach our Father in heaven with the love and trust of a child. In Mark 10:15 we read Christ's words: "Truly, I say to you, whoever does not receive the kingdom of God like a child shall not enter it."[3]

Faith is the first step into knowledge and through it, we learn to love and finally serve God. It is organic and grows when nurtured through prayer, knowledge, and sacrifice. Connecting with other faith-filled souls and studying inspiring examples of faith also strengthen this virtue. Faith takes work. When you enter a library, you actually have to pick up a book. Reading doesn't spontaneously occur as you walk through the door, any more than entering a restaurant means that you are eating. Faith is similar; it will draw you in, but requires effort to reach fulfillment.

Faith is not only about belief and trust; it is also about answering God's call and letting Him work through us. After a recent terrorist attack, a meme appeared that said "God isn't fixing this." It was true; He wasn't fixing our problems because we weren't letting Him work through us. We reflexively turn to God in prayer in times of trouble, which is right and good, but seldom listen for His answer, particularly when that answer requires something of us. Many ills in this world could be cured if we listened to the will of God and let Him work through us. To do so requires faith. When you find yourself discouraged by circumstances or events, pray to God for guidance and accept His desire to work through you. Faith is a willingness to be part of God's plan, even when we don't fully know or understand it.

A journey of faith is seldom a linear path, and numerous obstacles often impede progress. Counterfeit spirituality, with its misplaced trust in false gods, human power, material objects, or demonic summoning runs directly counter to faith. In the third book of the Bible we are warned: "Do not turn to mediums or wizards; do not seek them out, to be defiled by them: I am the Lord your God."[4] Doing so violates the first commandment that we shall worship God only. Other prohibited pseudo spiritualities include horoscopes, astrology, palm-reading, and divination, as they all express a desire to exert control over time and the human soul.[5] People who pursue curiosity in the occult often think they are dabbling out of interest or for fun, but end up jeopardizing their faith in God. You won't find the answers to life's questions in Ouija boards or Voodoo, so avoid them altogether. Nothing good has ever come from this pursuit.

Frequently, obstacles to faith emanate from within. Ask yourself, how many times must God request that you do His will? Many of us hear a voice that tells us: God can't possibly really want me to do that, I don't know how, I wouldn't be good, other people are better, I'm afraid to do that, I am afraid to fail, I am afraid to try, I don't know how to start, or the crux of all reasons, I don't want to do that. Answering God's call and casting your worries aside is not as easy as it sounds. It requires faith and trust when, instead, many times we are filled with doubt.

Doubt by itself doesn't present an insurmountable hurdle to faith. Very few souls have perfect faith, and we shouldn't question the veracity of our faith because of doubt. Faith untested is faith imperfect. Willful doubt is the turning away from the call that we know and hear in our hearts. When doubt becomes an unexplored roadblock, it does nothing but separate us from God. But ordinary doubt can have just the opposite effect. It can move us to look deeper for an answer that, in the end, leaves us with greater knowledge and more fervent faith. Uncertainty can cause us to reach out to God in prayer for answers, and can open our hearts and minds to His voice and His will. Do not let doubt worry you. Instead, welcome it as a blessing intended to draw you closer to God, and be open to His answer. Jesus reassured us: "Ask, and it will be given you; seek, and you will find; knock, and it will be opened to you. For every one who asks receives, and he who seeks finds, and to him who knocks it will be opened."[6]

Sometimes, people use doubt as an excuse to stop seeking. They can't overcome it in a timeframe that seems acceptable to them so they abandon the pursuit. In reality, each of us is on a different path and timeline. Some can do quick research to find resolution; others may take months, years, or even a lifetime. Understand the importance of seeking God with a humble and prayerful heart and He will take care of the rest.

Doubt is not the sole domain of the ordinary Christian. Many great saints and prophets had their own struggles with a faith that developed over time. In the Old Testament, God informed Moses of his role in delivering the people of Israel from Egypt. Moses protested with a litany of reservations: I am a nobody, whom am I supposed to say you are, they won't listen, they won't believe me, I'm not good with words. After exhausting his excuses, Moses listened to God's reassurances, including the many miracles God would empower Moses to perform. Taking all of God's words into consideration, Moses replied with: "Oh, my Lord, send, I pray, some other person."[7] He didn't want to answer God's explicit call; he'd rather have been left alone. How often do we respond to God with the words "send someone else"?

When the situation went from bad to worse for the Israelites, Moses then questioned God's judgment.[8] Moses didn't know the plan, and he didn't yet have the faith to trust fully in God. His belief was present, but his willingness to answer God's call and trust in God's plan were lacking, even though he had direct contact with God's words. Moses overcame his doubts, and as we know, went on to become one of the most important figures in salvation history.

Christ's own apostles had their doubts, and they had the advantage of knowing the living Christ as He walked beside, broke bread with, and taught them. While they were in a boat together and Christ was sleeping, a great storm arose. The apostles woke Him. He calmed the sea with His words and then asked them if they had any faith.[9]

Peter gave us a parallel example of failing faith when, in similar circumstances, the apostles saw Christ walking on the water. They were afraid they were seeing a ghost "And Peter answered him, "Lord, if it is you, bid me come to you on the water.""[10] Christ summoned Peter and as he reached the Lord, his faith failed him and he began to sink. "Jesus immediately reached out his hand and caught him, saying to him, "O man of little faith, why did you doubt?""[11] The failing of Peter's faith had one last act and that was to deny Christ three times during His passion.[12] Peter wept bitterly, yet Christ built His church on the rock of Peter who at the end had such great faith that he himself was willingly crucified for it.

The apostle Thomas's doubt was so great that it spawned the phrase "doubting Thomas." After the resurrection, Christ appeared to the apostles, but Thomas was not present. When the apostles told Thomas what had transpired, he famously proclaimed: "Unless I see in his hands the print of the nails, and place my finger in the mark of the nails, and place my hand in his side, I will not believe."[13] Eight days later, Christ came again and stood before the apostles. This time, Thomas was present and Christ beckoned him to remove his doubts by examining the wounds in His hands and side. "Thomas answered him, "My Lord and my God!" Jesus said to him, "Have you believed because you have seen me? Blessed are those who have not seen and yet believe.""[14] Thomas went on to become a saint, preaching the Gospel to many peoples. Doubt is not the enemy of faith. You can find many examples of saints who grappled with doubt which eventually led them to a stronger faith. Use those examples as encouragement as you grow in your own faith.

Just as the Bible provides a view of souls struggling with faith, it also offers examples of remarkably well-developed faith. Abraham was tested when God called on him to sacrifice his only son, Isaac. Abraham didn't understand the plan and was ready to slay his son when the angel of the Lord stopped him.[15] Abraham's display of obedience through faith stands as one of the greatest imaginable examples of faith. When the angel stopped Abraham from sacrificing Isaac, God was telling us, through him, that our faith is more important than our sacrifices.

Gideon is another Old Testament example of extraordinary faith.[16] The Israelites had been delivered into the hands of the Midianites for seven years. An angel of the Lord came to Gideon, and called on him to drive them out. Gideon gathered thirty-two thousand men, but God had a different plan, and Gideon ultimately went into battle with only three hundred men. God didn't want the Israelites claiming that the victory was theirs. His desire instead was to force Gideon to use so few fighters that the glory had to go to God. Gideon trusted in God and the Israelites were victorious. Trust in God, precisely when the odds are seemingly stacked against us, is when faith is most virtuous.

Other biblical examples of faith include St. John the Baptist, St. Stephen the first martyr, and St. Peter and St. Paul who, along with most of the apostles, gave their earthly lives for Christ. There have been martyrs throughout history whose courage is a testament to what is possible with true faith. Unfortunately, we are once again living through a time of martyrdom with many people, particularly in the Middle East, giving their lives for the cross. We can take solace that they are now in paradise and try to emulate their faith in our daily lives.

Faith has its own power, but not for those who seek power. The power of faith is the power of God and cannot be subjugated to man's will, but to God's will alone. It cannot be wielded as an instrument for self-aggrandizement or wealth creation. Still, faith has power to heal and to transform. Consider these words from Christ:

"And he said to her, "Daughter, your faith has made you well; go in peace, and be healed of your disease.""[17]

"Then Jesus answered her, "O woman, great is your faith! Be it done for you as you desire." And her daughter was healed instantly."[18]

"Then he touched their eyes, saying, "According to your faith be it done to you." And their eyes were opened."[19]

"And to the centurion Jesus said, "Go; be it done for you as you have believed." And the servant was healed at that very moment."[20]

In these cases, Christ pointed directly to faith as a means to heal. Healings did not stop when Christ ascended to heaven. The apostles continued to heal many,[21] and saints throughout history have also continued to heal the sick. Many people have been healed through visits to the various sites of Marian apparitions. Miracles, while great examples of faith and God's goodness, are rare and are not done for the recipient, but for the glory of God. Faith requires an acceptance of God's will whether it is through suffering or healing.

In the Gospel, Christ also called attention to the correlation between a lack of faith and the inability to heal. The apostles tried to heal an epileptic boy and could not, so the father brought the boy directly to Christ. Christ healed the boy and told the apostles they were unable to heal the child because of their lack of faith.[22] Likewise, this passage was written of Christ's time in Nazareth: "And he did not do many mighty works there, because of their unbelief."[23]

More significant and more common than bodily healing is the healing of the soul through faith. The body will die eventually but not the soul, and its health is infinitely more important. We learned in the last chapter that sometimes brokenness is necessary to lead a soul to God. We cannot overcome our fragile, sinful nature alone. The ill seek a physician and God is that healer, when approached through faith. A soul should never fear approaching God for healing. An old saying from an unknown author states: "Fear knocked at the door, faith answered, no one was there." This sentiment doesn't mean that if you have faith, there is nothing to fear. Even faith-filled people have fear, but when they face fear with faith, faith changes fear because it changes them.

Faith is powerful, but of the three theological virtues, it is not preeminent. From 1 Corinthians: "So faith, hope, love abide, these three; but the greatest of these is love."[24] Many non-Catholic Christians espouse an opinion that proclaiming belief in Christ once ensures your salvation forever–once saved, always saved. Put another way, they will tell you that you are saved by faith alone. This erroneous notion seems attractive both in its simplicity and in the lack of effort required on the part of the purportedly saved. It isn't Catholic and it isn't true. St. Paul stated clearly that love is more important than faith, so how could we be saved by something inferior? Unlike love, faith is not eternal. Once we enter into full communion with God, who is love, faith will pass away because we won't need it. We know too that faith isn't a one-time declaration and that it requires more than belief; it is a way of living. Additionally, St. Paul told us if you don't have love, you gain nothing.[25] In James, we read: "You see that a man is justified by works and not by faith alone."[26] That doesn't mean we are redeemed through our works, for only through the cross are we redeemed. We also don't earn our salvation but accept it, through our sustained rejection of sin and adherence to Christ.

This topic is too big to cover in this book, but you should be aware or most likely are already aware of it. Tim Staples of Catholic Answers has some very clear and concise essays on faith that you can find online. Look for them, and don't let the confidence of people who promote the "once saved, always saved perspective" undermine the truth. Their confidence stems from their sincerity and desire to bring souls to Christ. Admire their zeal and willingness to share their faith, but understand and avoid their error.

Like our non-Catholic brothers and sisters, we too are called to share our faith. Foremost, we must begin in our homes. Understanding the importance of your spouse's salvation should cause you to want to move heaven and earth to share your faith with him or her regularly. Spouses rarely begin at the same point on the faith continuum, and the stronger-willed partner will often draw the other toward their end. Unfortunately, sometimes the less devout or secular spouse will draw his or her partner away from God. This transformation can happen little by little, until the new norm is a life where God is relegated to the background, and subsequently, forgotten altogether. The truth of God's law and salvation don't change, but the individual does. If you are further along in your spiritual development, you are duty-bound to share your faith with your spouse. If your spouse is further along in the journey, commit to supporting him or her by participating and being open to learn.

When children are involved, both parents have a special responsibility to share and exemplify their Catholic faith. Too many marriages have one partner bearing the sole responsibility of educating the children and bringing them to Mass. Children immediately pick up on the mixed message. The absentee spouse either doesn't care enough for his or her own salvation to go to Mass, or doesn't believe any of it makes a difference. In these cases, less devout spouses must reflect on what fruit they wish to be known and what legacy they wish to leave behind. They must ask what could possibly be more important than their child's salvation. Rather than fostering a deeper love of God, prioritizing anything else before Him can foster indifference in the young people who look to their parents to model their own behavior. Christ said very directly: "Whoever receives one such child in my name receives me; but whoever causes one of these little ones who believe in me to sin, it would be better for him to have a great millstone fastened round his neck and to be drowned in the depth of the sea."[27]

If you are unmarried, discussing your faith with a potential partner before marrying is vital for your own salvation. A person who will attempt to lead you away from God should be ruled out because that isn't love. A secular or tepidly faithful person who will support you and your children in faith formation is less problematic, and may be open to discussing his or her own salvation. Practicing Catholics will make your faith life less stressful, set an example for your children, and grow with you in Christ. The dating stages of a relationship present an excellent opportunity to begin to draw a potential partner closer to Christ. Barring the death of your spouse or circumstances that could lead to an annulment, you have one chance at marriage, so you should choose a spouse very carefully.

Faith, in practice, is belief, trust, and acceptance of God's call, sharing, and struggle. It is difficult. We fear putting our lives in God's hands because we fear what He might ask of us. Saints who did so often had to suffer greatly in this world. We honor them now, but they were mocked when they lived and battled all types of physical pain and spiritual hardship. The next chapter will examine a virtue that makes it easier to approach God with the faith and trust necessary to accept His will.

Chapter 9: Humility

Humility is the invisible virtue because by its very nature, it dwells in secret, not making itself known. Humble people are gentle souls whose soft tread in this life is so easy to be around that we seek them out. We linger in their presence because we sense they are different, and we long to understand their quiet power. Marked by kindness, they are comfortable with themselves and with others. They know their place in this world and possess an inner peace that keeps them grounded.

While humility manifests itself in tangible ways to other creatures, it is first an interior disposition toward God. One definition of humility is: "The supernatural virtue by which one attains the correct perception of one's relationship with God... The attitude of humility is: "I am good only because of God's mercy." Humility counters pride and seeks to serve God and others."[1]

This sometimes-invisible virtue facilitates the rest. In St. Catherine's Dialogue we read God's teaching: "Every perfection and every virtue proceeds from charity, and charity is nourished by humility."[2] Through charity or love, as one of the three theological virtues, humility feeds the rest. Faith draws a soul toward God, but humility alters the approach, fostering reverence and holy fear that enable faith to grow. Humility is present when a soul hopes in the very mercy of God. Prudence is made possible when, through humility, a soul considers the will of God when making decisions. Again from the Dialogue of St. Catherine: "obedience soon dies in a soul deprived of this little virtue of humility."[3] Love puts God and others (for the sake of God) before one's self. The willingness to do so is rooted in a disposition of humility.

Returning to the example from a prior chapter, think of love as an operating system, running on the hardware of our souls. Mercy and other virtues are its applications and humility its power supply. Love alone is more essential, but without the quiet unseen flow of humility, it cannot power up. Humility allows us to see God as the perfect programmer of all things. For the entire system to run as intended, we must follow the Bible as our user guide. When we run across a bug, we submit a ticket (a prayer) to the programmer to get ourselves back on track. Humility teaches us that unlike technological bugs, the setbacks we run across in our spiritual life are universally user errors.

Like technology, life can sometimes be frustrating. The answers to life's challenges lie not with us but through God. What we do, that we consider good, comes from God and not from us. From 1 Corinthians: "So neither he who plants nor he who waters is anything, but only God who gives the growth."[4] When people struggle for answers in life, they sometimes heed the advice: "Give it to God." This admission, done in faith through humility, concedes God's power to change that which we alone cannot. God pours forth this power to help souls overcome their sinfulness. St. Paul said: "I can do all things in him who strengthens me."[5] When souls believe they cannot overcome a particular sin, they are correct; they cannot. Where souls can't, however, God can. Humbly submitting to Him provides fertile ground for His grace to enter souls and change them.

Beyond acceptance of grace and subjugation of sin, humility offers other freedoms as well. A humble soul no longer has to masquerade as perfect. The stress to conform to unattainable societal standards has no grip on the humble of heart. They rightly know that they must please God and meet His standards, not anyone else's. Forgotten are the pressures to style themselves as someone they are not. Instead, pleasing God is their chief concern. Humility frees people to ask for and receive help from others because they accept their own imperfections. As souls learn to see God in and value the gifts of others, they learn to recognize God and His gifts in themselves.

In humility we find freedom, but there are also many roadblocks. How we perceive God is how we receive God. Spiritual success is predicated on accepting that God is far superior to us and good and right in every way. Humility makes possible the acknowledgment that God's ways are so much greater than our ways. It provides us with the willingness to submit to His law, even when we don't fully comprehend its purpose. Pope Benedict XVI said "I know if I do not understand something that doesn't mean that it is wrong, but that I am too small for it."[6] If a soul were to perceive God's nature as only slightly more advanced than his or her own, the soul would become a law unto himself or herself instead of submitting to His will.

In our culture, submission to anyone or anything other than self runs counter to prevailing wisdom. Where totalitarian regimes emphasize the state's rights over submission to a higher power, western democracies emphasize individuality and individual rights over submission to a higher power. Secular education models will never teach the rightly ordered virtue of humility based on a person's relationship with God. In many cases, they work against it, through an over emphasis on self-esteem. Religious education programs largely or fully ignore this virtue, concentrating mainly on God's love for an individual rather than how to approach Him in His greatness. Mixed with a healthy dose of humility, honoring personal dignity and recognizing the overwhelming love that God has for each soul are worthy ideals. Absent humility, these values can engender an inflated and destructive sense of pride.

Pride is a funny word. Most of us have a good feeling when we hear it, but pride, first among the deadly sins, is an enabler of the rest. This vice rejects the supremacy of God and feeds hate in the same manner that humility nourishes love. Pride relies not on God but on self. As the guardian of all other sins, pride tells the sinner that man is greater than God, and an individual knows better the difference between right and wrong. Humility is invisible and cannot often be seen, but pride is blind and cannot see. Pride cannot recognize itself, or when it does, it attempts to present itself as a virtue. A soul with other vices present feels the pull of conscience, but pride stifles the voice of God and drowns it out. In one of St. Faustina's visions, Christ told her: "The greatest misery does not stop Me from uniting Myself to a soul, but where there is pride, I am not there."[7]

Pride is the tent in which all other vices dwell, the force field creating a seemingly impenetrable barrier that repels holiness. When pride establishes itself in a soul, it is very difficult to dislodge. This vice deceives a soul into believing that he or she is right and God and His church are wrong. In degrees, pride can create small rebellions, cafeteria Catholics, rejection, and ultimately, a hatred of God. Pride can also fool souls into believing that they are holier than they really are. St. John stated, "If we say we have no sin, we deceive ourselves, and the truth is not in us."[8]

Rather than nourishing holiness, pride seeks to feed itself by destroying it and devours goodness as its rations. Its primary concern with other souls is to diminish their importance in its own wake in a vain attempt to build itself up. We see pride manifest in gossip or singling people out for ridicule and insult. Current online discourse is filled with prideful people attacking not just each other's ideas, but each other. St. Thomas Aquinas wrote on civil discourse: "We must love them both, those whose opinions we share and those whose opinions we reject. For both have labored in the search for truth and both have helped us in the finding of it." [9] Humility, not pride, allows us to love those we disagree with and honor their value as human beings. Conversely, our current political leaders seem to have adopted community activist Saul D. Alinsky's tactics of ridicule and personal polarization. These destructive tactics have trickled down to ordinary citizens and infected the masses who demonize others in open expressions of hate, that people a generation ago would have found appalling. God's love and God's law have the strength to stand on their own and must be presented with love and holy compassion. Although as Catholics we cannot cede or negotiate the truth, we should not resort to denigrating those who haven't yet accepted God's call in their hearts.

Because pride can blind a soul, recognizing these examples is important in order to avoid them. Recognizing what is not pride is also important so we don't misjudge and avoid or accept situations unnecessarily. Self-satisfaction in a job well done is not a capital sin. Whether the task was mowing the lawn, finishing a project, or perhaps attaining some new level of achievement, you should feel good about an accomplishment. Reflect on it with gratitude to God for putting the opportunity before you and giving you the means to complete it. Gratitude is as sure a reflection of humility as ingratitude is a certain indication of pride.

Refusing to accept abusive treatment toward yourself or others is not pride. The use of physical, sexual, and verbal abuse is a way of denying, or attempting to force you to deny your own human dignity. That is disordered and sinful, and should be rejected. Humility helps us avoid being offended with every transgression, but never requires us to accept abusive behavior.

Even for the lack of attention that humility receives and the roadblocks before it, it remains one of the most endearing virtues. Stories of an underdog quietly persisting against long odds become wildly popular on social media, particularly when the subject had not drawn attention to himself or herself. We root for them in their courageous struggle, and often times, they receive widespread financial or spiritual support. Secular and Christian cultures intersect in admiration of humility, even if they don't both come from the same understanding of this virtue. This high regard for humility is why St. Mother Teresa was renowned and respected throughout the world. Humility is the common ground wherein all people can meet, if they can find their way to it.

Increasing humility in our own souls increases the opportunities to allow others to experience Christ through us. A beautiful way to nurture humility in our souls is to look for reflections of God in our world. When you encounter something magnificent, contemplate the vastness of God's nature. Some examples:

Mountains - God's majesty
Oceans or sands - God's infinite nature
Night sky - God's mystery
Sunsets - God's beauty
Newborn - God's sign of hope
Eucharist - God's love
DNA - God's intelligence

God's infinite nature is evident in His works if we take the time to consider them. Connecting with His power in this way can engender a rightly ordered sense of self through appreciation of God's greatness and splendor.

Failure is also a useful teacher of humility, particularly when we fail in spiritual endeavors. As humans, we are imperfect creatures. We fail much more often than we succeed. In baseball, a batter who fails six times out of ten is considered wildly successful. People fail much less often in their personal lives, yet they rarely find value in their lack of success. Failure's silver lining is an understanding of our limitations and an increase in humility. It cultivates a reliance on God to achieve success in the future and to accept failure when we must.

The virtue of humility can likewise mature through success. Achievement gives the soul an opportunity to be grateful for the assistance of God and others. It puts a timeline to the work required for success, and a perspective on how many people were involved. This perspective is true even in seemingly individual achievements. Success that takes the form of service to others has the ability to make all parties feel humble. A service of great love can help people appreciate their own role in something much greater than themselves because the act is so big.

One of the best ways to increase in humility is to seek examples to emulate. No book called *The Pride of the Saints* was ever written because pride precludes saintly life. So look to the saints as some of the finest examples of humility. God requested Our Blessed Mother, foremost among the saints, to carry and care for His only Son. Ever God's faithful servant, Mary had an immediate affirmative response and submission to God's will that were made with perfect humility. St. John the Baptist lived a simple life in the wilderness, calling people to repent. When people questioned if he were the Christ, "John answered them all, "I baptize you with water; but he who is mightier than I is coming, the thong of whose sandals I am not worthy to untie; he will baptize you with the Holy Spirit and with fire.""[10] When Christ presented Himself to John for Baptism, out of humility John didn't want to comply, but submitted to Christ's will nevertheless.

The Incarnation in which Christ assumed human nature[11] provides an unparalleled act of humility. That Christ, the Second Person of the Trinity, became man to walk among us is incomprehensible. Knowing who He was, how He lived His life, and the sacrifice He made for us offers a profound and perfect example of humility. Christ wasn't born in a palace surrounded by servants; He was born in a stable and then placed in a manger surrounded by barnyard animals. We've romanticized the scene and sanitized it of its true grittiness. Imagine you or your spouse were pregnant and about to give birth. Now envision, instead of grabbing your overnight bag and driving to the hospital, you had to ride a bicycle to some random barn, sight unseen. Most of us won't stay in a hotel without checking online reviews. But in this scenario, you'd be in a stable with the accompanying sights and smells to bring your child into the world. We wouldn't want to do that for our child because it isn't good enough, but it was good enough for God's only Son.

Christ told us "the Son of man came not to be served but to serve"[12] and He lived His life in that accord. When He washed the feet of the apostles, the task was one normally consigned to servants. Today, the chore would be akin to Christ appearing at our door and offering to clean our floors and bathrooms. We'd be horrified, and we'd object. The apostles were, too, but Christ came to lead by example, and His love was so great that He was willing to humble Himself for the good of man. As foretold in Psalm 25: "He leads the humble in what is right, and teaches the humble his way."[13] If He was willing to do this, what should we be willing to do?

The words of the Centurion are another example of humility that we can find in the Bible, and ones we memorialize at every Mass. The Centurion's servant was ill and he begged Christ to heal his servant. Christ told him that He would come and heal the servant, "But the centurion answered him, "Lord, I am not worthy to have you come under my roof; but only say the word, and my servant will be healed."[14] Humility and faith, as mentioned earlier in the chapter, are a potent combination and Christ healed the servant at that moment.

Souls are called to humility in Scripture: "Do nothing from selfishness or conceit, but in humility count others better than yourselves."[15] This knowledge and these examples of humility can help us live more humbly. When struggling with perceived injustices, humility can help restrain us from saying or doing something not in line with our Catholic faith. Wanting to mete out some type of immediate revenge to let people know you are not to be trifled with is easy. Reflecting on the sorrowful mysteries of the Holy Rosary and considering how the Maker of the world did just the opposite is astonishing. The insults and brutality hurled His way were the pinnacle of injustice, yet He bore them without once striking back. Realizing that Christ could have punished the soldiers with a simple thought makes His restraint all the more remarkable. Christ set a perfect example for us when we bear sufferings and trials. How will we respond to those trials? Choosing revenge isn't motivated by justice, but by a love of reputation or pride. Humility can counteract that impulse.

Humility in practice leaves the judgments that are rightly God's with God and avoids the presumption of usurping His authority. We witness, God judges. He gave us the truth and our job as Christians is to bear witness to it, whether people listen or not. We can witness by example, through prayer or music, in conversation, by a holy life, or in the written word as I am doing now. However, we don't judge and should never declare that someone is going to hell or has gone to hell. We cannot know the state of someone's soul. We can know observable behaviors that put them in grave danger and encourage them to change, but only God can judge the condition of a soul. There have been instances of saints to whom the state of another person's soul has been divinely revealed. This insight was granted in order to help the sinner find their way back to God's will. These saints were the exception; we are not. As mere humans, who would want to carry the burden of knowing the true state of someone's soul? If the soul were in a holy and unblemished state, there would be great joy. If the opposite were true and he or she was in a damned state, the knowledge would cause tremendous heartache and pain.

Living in humility also leads us to an appreciation that everyone processes thoughts differently. Don't expect too much from others, and don't expect people to understand your perspective unless you are willing to risk sharing something of yourself to help them understand. The courage to be vulnerable is rooted in humility.

Humility is critical to the well-being of a soul. If you choose to focus on only one virtue, choose humility. It nurtures love, and love leads to all other virtues. Humility opens a heart to communion with God. It enables the quiet contemplation with which we enter prayer. In fact, the *Catechism of the Catholic Church* stipulates: "*humility* is the foundation of prayer."[16] We often think only of vocal or ritual prayer, but the next chapter examines multiple ways to commune with God.

Chapter 10: Prayer

While working in Boston, I decided to start praying the rosary during my train ride in to the city. This devotion soon became a regular part of my morning routine. When I switched jobs, I continued praying in the car during my new commute. My prayers included a list of regular intentions that would change from time to time and occasionally, a rosary for a single petition. During one dark winter commute, I randomly began thinking about horrific fiery auto accidents. I imagined how painful dying in that manner must be, and how much suffering burn victims endured when they survived such a wreck. That morning, I decided to pray a rosary, requesting that Our Blessed Mother obtain from God the favor of sparing one family from such a fate. The commute was longer than the rosary; I finished praying, put the beads down, and flipped to CNN on the satellite radio. The very first story was about a Good Samaritan who had pulled a family from a fiery crash. They'd sustained only minor injuries. I turned the radio off, surprised to have heard what would generally have been a local story on a national station, but more surprised by the account itself. The report certainly could have been a coincidence, but I believe it was something else. I believe God was letting me know that prayer matters. Perhaps the family in the car was praying for deliverance. The citizen hero could possibly have been praying for an act of mercy that he could perform that day. Maybe my prayers hadn't made any difference in that case at all. Maybe my only role was to receive the message that prayer matters.

Prayer matters a great deal. While not a substitute for weekly Mass attendance, prayer is vital to the health and spiritual development of a soul. Imagining how a soul could move forward without regular prayer is difficult. In prayer, we humbly raise our hearts and minds to God, seeking to unify them with His being and His will. Prayer is an act of open

111

communication and communion with the Almighty. Through it, we develop openness to God's rightful place in our lives. Sin begets sin, but prayer begets holiness. The more often we pray, the closer to God we become. The closer to God we become, the more inclined we are to do His will. Prayer is a counterbalance to sin.

God continually calls us to prayer, and that call is not a New Testament construct. The foundation of prayer is evident as early as the first book of the Old Testament when God called to Adam in the garden.[1] From Adam, Abraham, Moses, and Samuel, to Isaiah and all of the prophets through to the Psalms, God repeatedly called His people to conversation, to communion, to prayer. In the Book of Exodus, God sets guidelines for the priesthood, altar, Sabbath, feast days, the tabernacle, and a place of worship all oriented toward communal prayer. In Leviticus, God instructs His people to make offerings for sin, thanksgiving, atonement, and restitution. In 2 Chronicles, God told Solomon: "if my people who are called by my name humble themselves, and pray and seek my face, and turn from their wicked ways, then I will hear from heaven, and will forgive their sin and heal their land."[2]

In the New Testament, Christ Himself prayed repeatedly and told us, "Therefore I tell you, whatever you ask in prayer, believe that you receive it, and you will."[3] Paul's letters are filled with exhortations to pray and to "pray constantly."[4] St. James told us we should pray when we are suffering, cheerful, or sick.[5]

We are clearly and repeatedly called to prayer, both explicitly and by example, but why? Why does God want us to pray, even though He knows all of our needs before we ask? Fundamentally, God's call to prayer is rooted in our creation as outlined in the very first paragraph of the *Catechism of the Catholic Church*. "God, infinitely perfect and blessed in himself, in a plan of sheer goodness freely created man to make him share in his own blessed life. For this reason, at every time and in every place, God draws close to man."[6] Recall from chapter four that God desires all people to be saved, and prayer enables the disposition necessary to receive His word, His will, and His grace. His wish that we share in His love begins not in heaven, but on Earth through prayer. Prayer is an expression of our love to the Trinity and from the Trinity back to us.

Additionally, prayer declares our reliance on God for all things and through it, we acknowledge His supreme authority over us. The Chaplet of Divine Mercy prayer is an excellent example: "Eternal Father, I offer you the Body and Blood, Soul and Divinity of Your Dearly Beloved Son, Our Lord, Jesus Christ, in atonement for our sins and those of the whole world." We know that Christ is the one who offered those sacrifices in atonement for our sins, not us; so reciting those words may seem odd. We convey by them an acknowledgment of the full and complete sacrifice of Christ, and accept that through that sacrifice, He redeemed the world and each of us individually. We are accepting, owning, and internalizing that truth when we pray this chaplet. Requesting something from God through prayer is another example of a soul acknowledging the sovereignty of God.

When Catholics hear the word prayer, they often think first of our most common prayers, such as the Our Father, the Hail Mary, or the Glory Be to the Father. Prayer is much broader in scope and expression than the prayers we first learned as children. The *Catechism of the Catholic Church* identifies the five following types of prayer: blessing and adoration, petition, intercession, thanksgiving, and praise.[7]

Our Sunday Visitor's Catholic Dictionary contains this about blessings: "In the Scriptures, blessings express God's generosity, favor, and unshakable love for His children."[8] We ask for God's blessings for ourselves and share them with others in word and in deed. Creatures cannot add anything to God so when we bless the Lord, we mean to say that we hold Him blessed and revered in our hearts and minds. Adoration, likewise, holds God far above all of creation. A supreme love expressed through worship and glorification, adoration is reserved for God alone.

Petition is an innate form of prayer by design. When we are in trouble, we reach out to God and ask Him to help us. We move toward Him because we cannot find fulfillment in any finite creature or means. This petitioning is the most likely gateway through which non-religious people begin to seek God. Hearing a person testify that they weren't the praying type until they were in real trouble and called out to God for help is not uncommon. Rightly ordered, a prayer of petition begins by asking for forgiveness and mercy. A humble start from an unworthy petitioner shifts the soul more quickly toward God. Praying for yourself is morally acceptable and beneficial. Every need, in accordance with God's will, can be addressed through petition.

Closely related to petition are prayers of intercession, through which we pray for someone else's benefit. To do so is one of the spiritual acts of mercy. Intercession also happens when other people pray for us. Scripture contains many examples of and directives to intercessory prayer. Moses prayed for the Israelites when they angered God with their sinfulness.[9] The people asked the prophet Samuel to pray for them.[10] In the Book of Job, we read, "And the Lord restored the fortunes of Job, when he had prayed for his friends; and the Lord gave Job twice as much as he had before."[11] St. James instructs us to pray for one another.[12] St. Paul asked the people to pray for him that he might boldly proclaim the Gospel.[13] In 1 Timothy, St. Paul clearly implores intercessory prayer: "First of all, then, I urge that supplications, prayers, intercessions, and thanksgivings be made for all men."[14]

In this spirit of intercession, we pray to the saints. Non-Catholics sometimes confuse requests for intercession with worship. Catholics, as all Christians, worship only the Father, Son, and Holy Spirit. When we pray the rosary, we are

114

asking Mary to pray for us, not worshipping her as a deity. We love and honor (venerate) Our Blessed Mother and other saints for their holy lives and examples, but do not remotely equate them with the Trinity.

The dead, although separated from our physical world, remain connected to us spiritually. Even though we can no longer speak in earthly ways to the saints in heaven, we can still communicate with them through prayer. Our one church contains three distinct groups. The Church Militant consists of the souls still struggling on Earth. Their final destination has not yet been determined. Souls in purgatory, the Church Suffering, are souls whose fate has been determined, but they still must be purified before entering heaven. Souls in heaven belong to the Church Triumphant. Like the souls in the Church Suffering, their fate has been irreversibly determined but unlike them, they no longer face a separation from God. All souls in heaven are considered saints because they no longer have any attachment to sin. Their will is in full communion with the will of God. We don't know the identity of all of the souls in heaven, but we know the identity of some. The church on Earth recognizes as saints those souls who lived a life of extraordinary charity and virtue in complete accord with God's will. Their prayers are powerful because their love of God and denial of self were powerful. Asking them to pray for us is no different from asking an earthly soul for an intercessory prayer. If they obtain a favor or even a miracle for the Church Militant, they do so only through our Lord Jesus Christ, and not of their own volition.

Thanksgiving is the fourth type of prayer. It has its own holiday, but is often ignored in daily prayer life. When life is going well, we seems to forget God easily. When Christ healed ten lepers, only one returned to give thanks.[15] Our natural inclination is to seek God when we are hurting, and sometimes we become less attentive to His goodness in our lives when we are doing well. Truthfully, a spirit of gratitude toward God is necessary in both good and bad times. St. Paul taught that we must "give thanks in all circumstances; for this is the will of God in Christ Jesus for you."[16] Loving God and appreciating His goodness through difficult times is an indication of a soul who understands and accepts the rightly ordered relationship between Creator and creature. Prayers of thanksgiving in all circumstances are the culmination of humility in a soul. Imagine the transformation that could be achieved in a soul who began every prayer with the words "Thank you, Lord."

The last prayer type is praise. Praise is the prayer that is filled with joy. Its beauty lies in the response of a soul to God's greatness and the reflection of God's wisdom and goodness on a soul. According to the *Catechism of the Catholic Church*: "It lauds God for his own sake and gives him glory, quite beyond what he does, but simply because HE IS."[17] Praise motivates not God but the soul who expresses it. It witnesses to the world the Glory of God. All prayer is beautiful, but in praise we tell God, when all else falls away, you are Holy God, Holy Mighty One, and Holy Immortal One.

These five types of prayer can be expressed in three fundamental ways. The first expression of prayer is vocal prayer. Vocal prayer begins in our youth with traditional prayers spoken out loud. During the Mass, the spoken prayers, Scripture readings, and hymns are all examples of vocal prayer. Vocal prayer need not be audible; the formation of words in our minds is also considered vocal prayer.

Vocal prayer leads to the second expression of prayer, meditation. The *Catechism of the Catholic Church* states this about meditation: "Meditation is above all a quest. The mind seeks to understand the why and how of the Christian life, in order to adhere and respond to what the Lord is asking."[18] Remaining focused in meditation is often difficult, but concentration improves with repetition. Meditation can be inspired through the reading of Scripture, the writings of the saints, through vocal prayers such as the Holy Rosary, or any other means that help us reflect on the meaning of our Catholic faith. Before beginning meditation, it's good to establish the practice of offering a vocal prayer of petition to the Holy Spirit seeking the gifts of wisdom and understanding.

The final expression of prayer is contemplative prayer. In contemplation we spend time silently experiencing God's presence. We are attentive to His fully encompassing love. We listen without responding. We find peace in His company. Eucharistic Adoration is the finest form of contemplation. Vocal and meditative prayers before the Holy Eucharist are enormously beneficial, but cannot match the intensity of contemplation. Contemplation can happen anywhere. You can put this book down right now, close your eyes, and feel God present with you. Contemplation can last hours or even for a moment. At Mass, when the priest consecrates the Host, consider bowing your head and saying quietly, "my Lord and my God." When he consecrates the wine, pray, "my Lord Jesus Christ." In both instances, simply acknowledge God's presence in quiet contemplation. Take advantage of those moments when and where you can. Replace the old adage that tells you to stop and smell the roses with one that says stop and feel God's presence.

Knowing the different types and expressions of prayer helps broaden our understanding of our prayer life, but another ingredient is necessary for optimal prayer. Prayer must come from the heart with fervor and intention. It can be simple or complex, but it must be authentic. Don't be troubled if on occasion or even for extended periods you feel as though your prayers are flat. Going through periods of dry prayer is not uncommon, but maintaining a steadfast commitment to praying is important. Twice in the Gospel according to Luke, Christ taught His listeners to remain steadfast in prayer and not to lose heart.[19] When you find yourself struggling in your prayer life, read these Scripture passages and let Christ's encouragement carry you forward. If you fail, remember always that we pray not because we are saints, but because we are sinners.

With the basics of prayer covered, consider one of the most profound examples of prayer found in Scripture–Christ in the garden of Gethsemane. The human Christ knew how painful His coming torturous death would be. He prayed that the cup pass Him by, that there be some other way. Even knowing of the pain that He would have to endure, Christ said, "Father, if thou art willing, remove this cup from me; nevertheless not my will, but thine, be done."[20] His will was so perfectly aligned to the will of the Father that He was prepared to submit to torture and death. As we know, the Father did not grant Christ's request. Through His Divinity, Christ knew the Scriptures would be fulfilled but He, the perfect petitioner, prays a perfect prayer as an example for us. Although the cup didn't pass Christ by, the Father answered the Son by sending an angel from heaven to strengthen Him. God hears our prayers and answers them, but not always with the answer for which we had hoped. He didn't answer Christ's prayer the way we might have expected, yet three days later, the world was changed forever because of it. We too must accept the will of the Father, even when our prayer doesn't work out as we had hoped. God knows His plan for each of us and we have to trust in His goodness.

God also does answer many prayers in the way we request when our human will is aligned with His divine will. Do not be discouraged or lose heart when your prayers appear as though they have gone unanswered. God sends other answers and signs, but we must be open to them in order to see them. Maybe our answer won't be healing but strength and faith. Also, you are unlikely to receive visions or visitations from angels to help you determine the will of God. Through prayer, knowledge, and counsel though, you can still discern it.

The first priority of prayer is getting started. Prayer has a way of drawing souls in deeper over time, so don't be afraid to begin modestly. Ideally, a good framework to begin with is morning prayer, evening prayer, and prayer before meals. Over time, you may find yourself delving into devotions such as novenas, the Holy Rosary, the Chaplet of Divine Mercy, the Stations of the Cross, or any number of other options. So many people need prayers and you will find no shortage of special intentions for which to pray. Consider praying for the following: the unemployed, anyone suffering, souls in purgatory, the clergy and all religious brothers and sisters, your local priests, vocations, conversions, those who have suffered a death in the family, homeless, hungry, victims of violence or domestic abuse, those struggling with addiction, etc. Pray too for the health, safety, and salvation of yourself and your family. Try different types and expressions of prayer. Prayer is a way of life, and everything, if done with the will of God in mind, can be offered to our Creator as a prayer.

Purchase a good Catholic prayer book to stimulate ideas. Commit to praying daily and over time, you will notice a difference in yourself and how you view the rest of the world. Below are some beautiful and less common prayers to consider using.

The Jesus Prayer
Lord Jesus Christ, Son of God, have mercy on me a sinner.

Act of Contrition
O my God, I am heartily sorry for having offended Thee, and I detest all my sins, because I dread the loss of heaven, and the pains of hell; but most of all because they offend Thee, my God, Who art all-good and deserving of all my love. I firmly resolve, with the help of Thy grace, to confess my sins, to do penance, and to amend my life.
Amen.

Act of Faith
O my God, I firmly believe that you are one God in three divine Persons, Father, Son, and Holy Spirit. I believe that your divine Son became man and died for our sins, and that He will come to judge the living and the dead. I believe these and all the truths which the holy Catholic Church teaches, because you have revealed them, who can neither deceive nor be deceived.
Amen.

Act of Hope
O my God, relying on your infinite mercy and promises, I hope to obtain pardon of my sins, the help of your grace, and life everlasting, through the merits of Jesus Christ, my Lord and Redeemer.
Amen.

Act of Love
O my God, I love you above all things with my whole heart and soul, because you are all good and worthy of all my love. I love my neighbor as myself for the love of you. I forgive all who have injured me and I ask pardon of those whom I have injured.
Amen.

Prayer to St. Michael
St. Michael the Archangel, defend us in battle.
Be our protection against the wickedness and snares of the Devil. May God rebuke him, we humbly pray,
and do thou, O Prince of the Heavenly Hosts,
by the power of God, cast into hell Satan, and all the evil spirits, who prowl about the world seeking the ruin of souls.
Amen.

Hail, Holy Queen

Hail, Holy Queen, Mother of Mercy, our life, our sweetness and our hope! To thee do we cry, poor banished children of Eve. To thee do we send up our sighs, mourning and weeping in this valley of tears! Turn, then, most gracious advocate, thine eyes of mercy toward us, and after this, our exile, show unto us the blessed fruit of thy womb, Jesus.
O clement, O loving, O sweet Virgin Mary.
V. Queen of the most Holy Rosary, pray for us.
R. That we may be made worthy of the promises of Christ.

St. Ignatius Prayer

Teach us, good Lord,
To serve you as you deserve;
To give, and not to count the cost;
To fight, and not to heed the wounds;
To toil, and not to seek for rest;
To labor, and not to ask for any reward,
Save that of knowing that we do your will.

In the previous three chapters, we've reflected on how to approach God with faith and humility, and through prayer. In the last chapter of this section and of the book, we consider a beautiful virtue with which we should approach God, and in which we should live our lives.

Chapter 11: Hope

When we think again of Christ in the garden of Gethsemane, who are we in the story? Most of us start in a place where we aren't yet in the garden. We start as the soldiers who ignorantly came to arrest Christ, not knowing who He was or fully understanding the ramifications of their actions. Then, through knowledge and prayer, we become the disciples. Disciples who followed Christ, but even the best of whom could not stay present with Him as they drifted off to sleep, leaving Him to suffer alone. What great hope there is in knowing that the apostles of Christ would soon become fearless leaders and champions of His message. Christ took ignorant and sleeping men and through grace, turned them into reflections of His word in this world. No matter what state you find yourself in today, Christ can pick you up where you are and do great things with you if you wake from your sleep. Today is never too late, no matter what has come before, but don't wait until tomorrow because tomorrow is never guaranteed. Cast aside all doubt, fear, and worry and ask Christ to start working on you, so that He can eventually work through you. This is hope.

In the *Catechism of the Catholic Church* we read: "Hope is the theological virtue by which we desire the kingdom of heaven and eternal life as our happiness, placing our trust in Christ's promises and relying not on our own strength, but on the help of the grace of the Holy Spirit."[1] Hope looks toward heaven and the soul's reward. Unlike presumption, which expects reward through a sense of entitlement, hope presumes nothing, but humbly believes in the saving power of God's grace. St. Ambrose of Milan wrote about hope: "It is not insolent arrogance but an innocent conscience which seeks a reward from Him whom you serve."[2] Humility feeds hope and protects it from becoming presumption.

Our encounter with each of the three theological virtues should differ in approach. Faith is to be embraced, love is to be accepted, but hope must be seized. Grab hold of it and never let it go. Hope can be your bridge when faith fails you. Hope will remind you of God's goodness when you don't feel love. Hope focuses you on the higher gifts. It's a life preserver in a sea of anguish. It is sometimes the last line of defense against loss. Hope is a gateway to mercy. It trusts in the constancy of God. From the Book of Isaiah: "The grass withers, the flower fades; but the word of our God will stand for ever."[3] A life lived in hope smoothes the valleys of despair. When you feel abandoned or alone, hope reminds you of God's ever-present nature. Consider this excerpt from Acts: "In him we live and move and have our being."[4] St. Cyril of Jerusalem wrote: "Every laborer is prepared to endure the toils if he looks forward to the reward of these toils. But they who labor without reward—their soul is exhausted with their body."[5] Hope maintains a soul's focus on God, providing comfort to the afflicted and reminding us of the transitory nature of our earthly presence.

Hope's reliance on God's help makes all things possible through Him. When sin seems to have a stranglehold on us and we think we can't defeat it, we are correct. We are correct, that is, if we attempt to conquer sin alone. Rely instead on God, through a hope enabled by humility to ensure a victory. Let God's grace be your finishing agent. Know that you cannot do it yourself. Never be discouraged in your struggle against sin. Never give up. That voice inside that tells you to quit, the effort is not worth it, the task is impossible, or you shouldn't bother, is not the voice of hope from God; it is the voice of despair, and it emanates from a much darker place. The stronger the voice of despair becomes, the closer you are to victory. The voice of discouragement may not always originate internally; it may emerge as advice from family or friends. Hope is powerful enough to overcome those voices. A soul who remains steadfast in hope may sway external voices and draw them closer toward God.

But hope is not a miracle drug, nor is prayer a magical incantation that yields immediate results. We struggle against sin and against our nature. The narrative that people who commit themselves to God immediately stop sinning and become saintly is false. Some saint-like people are on Earth, but most of us are trying to improve one day at a time. We pray not because we are saints, but because we are sinners. Humility teaches us that we need God, and hope tells us that relying on Him to help us reach heaven is rightly ordered.

Signs of hope can bring encouragement along our journey. The accounts of two of the greatest saints are well-known stories of hope. St. Peter, whose faith was strong but faltering, became the first pope. He didn't become perfect when he began following Christ; he worked at improving day by day, fed by the word of God and the example of Christ. St. Paul, who persecuted Christians, became one of the most important church leaders and through him, we receive much of the New Testament. At the time, that such a man could ever become a saint seemed impossible, yet he did. Perhaps God chose Paul specifically to illustrate that no matter how grave our sin, there is healing hope and mercy in the arms of Christ. Regardless of how far we have strayed, we can now rejoin our Savior and walk with Him from this point forward.

The sacraments of the church provide signs of hope in God's help. They provide us with grace and renewal throughout our lives. Baptism removes the stain of original sin. Confession is a constant renewal of the state of grace necessary to accept salvation. The Holy Eucharist strengthens us on our journey in a full sharing of Christ's sacrifice. Confirmation confers the gifts of the Holy Spirit, fortifying our souls for the battle. Holy Orders and Matrimony bestow graces to assist in holy living for a soul's chosen vocation. Anointing of the Sick provides grace to those suffering or near death. Reception of any of the sacraments is an expression of hope in God for His aid on our journey toward heaven. Our response, in particular to the two we can participate in regularly, the Holy Eucharist and Confession, can become an example of hope to others.

Hope, like love and faith, is given to souls to be shared. We can share examples of hope through our participation in the sacraments, and in other ways as well. Hope can manifest itself in an encouraging word, the promise to pray for someone's well-being, or in gifts such as prayer books or inspiring quotes. Most often, hope is shared when we share our faith. In sharing our faith, we are witnessing that we have found something beautiful. We desire the same good for our neighbor and believe it is possible through hope.

The work we undertake to align our will to God's will is just the first step. We must invite others to do the same. When you love someone, sharing the news of that love is only natural. Whether the object of our affection is a potential spouse, a newborn child, or even a new pet, we share pictures, post updates, and tell stories of our love. Do we feel at least that strongly about God? Will the enthusiasm of our relationship with Him be evident? God, who is even more intimately a part of us, who breathed our very life into us, doesn't always get the same recognition. How would you answer the old question: "If you were arrested and charged with being a Catholic, would there be enough evidence to convict you?" Sometimes, people see Christians as trying to convert them to build the size of their "club." That motive is not true for most, and we must ensure that it's not true for us. When we reach out to someone, that outreach should come from a place of love and genuine concern for their long-term happiness and salvation.

Christ shared a parable about a man who was going on a journey and called his servants to look after his talents.[6] A talent was a unit of currency equivalent to fifteen years' wages. To one servant, he gave five talents. To the second, he gave two talents and to the last servant, he gave one. Each of the first two servants doubled the master's money through investments, but the third servant buried the talent entrusted to him to keep it safe. When the master returned, he rewarded the first two servants and cast the third out of his house. His expectation was that each would use his talents to bring back more. We are the servants in this parable and Christ is the master. The purpose of life is to make a choice, and once we have chosen to serve Christ, He expects us to increase the yield with the talents He gave us. He's telling us through this parable to help bring more souls to Him.

Catholics particularly struggle with evangelization. We care quietly and privately about the salvation of others, but aren't universally willing to risk the hostile stare by being vocal about our faith. Sharing means receiving pushback, and Catholics can often be a very reserved and polite crew. The acceptance of Catholics by the mainstream culture took many decades and there seems an unwillingness to put that in jeopardy. Many Catholics believe remaining inwardly focused is much easier than inviting inevitable conflict by openly expressing faith, but that reluctance is not what Christ demands of us. Truly our faith is countercultural, and conflict between faith and the prevailing culture is inevitable. That conflict is also indicative of well-ordered faith formation.

The concepts of freedom and free will have been distorted into an ever-expanding definition that accepts any sinful behavior, as long as the soul is purportedly only hurting himself or herself. Believing that what happens to a neighbor doesn't matter, as long as you personally are in a state of grace, is not acceptable to God. That attitude shows a lack of love for both neighbor and for God. Catholics and other Christians are sometimes intimidated into silence, and certain segments of the population have attempted to shift the terminology from "freedom of religion" to "freedom to worship." Freedom of religion puts the evangelization of souls in the public square, but freedom to worship confines the Word of God to private places. Our duty is to reject the silencing of our faith and continue to invite others to accept Christ.

If you could save someone from some impending disaster that you knew was imminent, would you do or say nothing out of fear that you might offend? Consider a friend who doesn't want to bother shoveling out his exhaust vent in the winter. The effort is too much trouble and he doesn't really understand the consequences, so he doesn't take any precautions. You see the neglect happening and remain silent. The next day when your friend has died, you're left with what? Your pride? Your reputation? You're not left with your friendship and your friend isn't left with his life. That life on Earth was going to end one way or another. How much more tragic would the situation have been if your friend lost his life forever, for eternity? How complicit would you be? The situation can get even worse. Not warning people is bad, but encouraging them to remain in sin is worse. Doing so is essentially approving of their death.

Three years passed before people got weary of Christ and killed Him. They didn't want to hear His message and those in power didn't want to give up power, even to the truth. Christ spoke the truth and society tried to stop Him from the onset. He spoke the truth and died for us. Will we speak for Him and in doing so endure much less than death? When we meet Him again, will we be able to look at Him and say that we spoke up for Him?

Thinking of using our talents to lead others to the salvation of Christ can be overwhelming, especially if you begin to worry about the whole world. Don't. Let God take care of the world. Beginning at home and with people you know is generally more effective. As you look for occasions to share your faith, please understand that turning every conversation into an evangelization attempt is generally ineffective. That may work for some, but many people will just avoid you. Instead, pray for opportunities and stay in tune with the will of God. You will find surprising openings that you hadn't noticed before. Remember, souls are seeking fulfillment and will be more receptive than you might expect. Share encouraging stories with Catholic friends, no matter how small the victory may seem. Perhaps you'll see someone who hadn't been close to God make the sign of the cross after you pray for him or her. Maybe you will find someone willing to read an article or book you share. You never know what will touch a certain soul.

We are not all called to evangelize in the same way, so you don't have to become an instant extrovert to answer God's call. We can look to Scripture for guidance. "Now there are varieties of gifts, but the same Spirit; and there are varieties of service, but the same Lord; and there are varieties of working, but it is the same God who inspires them all in every one. To each is given the manifestation of the Spirit for the common good."[7] God can work through talents like writing, music, conversation, prayer, Bible study groups, religious vocations, religious education teachers, works of mercy, and anything else that witnesses to His love and draws souls closer to Him. We don't all have to become street evangelists to answer God's call to share His faith, hope, and love. Part of your spiritual journey is to discover the beautiful way that He will work through you. Reflect on these magnificently encouraging words from Christ: "You are the light of the world. A city set on a hill cannot be hid. Nor do men light a lamp and put it under a bushel, but on a stand, and it gives light to all in the house. Let your light so shine before men, that they may see your good works and give glory to your Father who is in heaven."[8]

As youngsters, we memorized basic prayers and learned fundamental facts about our faith. I attempted to weave pieces of our faith together to illustrate a straightforward, but more comprehensive picture than you may have had in the past. The closer you draw to God, the bigger the tapestry you will find, and it will be more beautiful to you. Pursue that beauty. God doesn't expect you to be perfect, but

He wants you to keep trying. Avoid sin, but follow the more successful strategy of seeking and then living God's will. The will of God is your goal; sin is the obstacle. Look further out and the obstacles will be easier to dodge. Start as simply as acknowledging that He is in charge, He is greater than we are, and love of Him must triumph over love of self. Really, that last piece says it all. When we put love of God before love of self, we turn away from false pride and toward true contrition. Then, we throw ourselves into His mercy and let Him do the rest.

In closing, I share my favorite Bible passage; the parable of the sower.

> ""Listen! A sower went out to sow. And as he sowed, some seed fell along the path, and the birds came and devoured it. Other seed fell on rocky ground, where it had not much soil, and immediately it sprang up, since it had no depth of soil; and when the sun rose it was scorched, and since it had no root it withered away. Other seed fell among thorns and the thorns grew up and choked it, and it yielded no grain. And other seeds fell into good soil and brought forth grain, growing up and increasing and yielding thirtyfold and sixtyfold and a hundredfold." And he said, "He who has ears to hear, let him hear."
>
> And when he was alone, those who were about him with the twelve asked him concerning the parables. And he said to them, "Do you not understand this parable? How then will you understand all the parables? The sower sows the word. And these are the ones along the path, where the word is sown; when they hear, Satan immediately comes and takes away the word which is sown in them. And these in like manner are the ones sown upon rocky ground, who, when they hear the word, immediately receive it

with joy; and they have no root in themselves, but endure for a while; then, when tribulation or persecution arises on account of the word, immediately they fall away. And others are the ones sown among thorns; they are those who hear the word, but the cares of the world, and the delight in riches, and the desire for other things, enter in and choke the word, and it proves unfruitful. But those that were sown upon the good soil are the ones who hear the word and accept it and bear fruit, thirtyfold and sixtyfold and a hundredfold.'""[9]

This parable really challenges us to think about how we approach the Gospel as a choice. The decision is an active one and we should think about it carefully. Thoughtfully consider what kind of ground you will be. Will you internalize the Word of God before Satan snatches it away? Will you accept the Word with excitement that flares up and then dissipates as culture and peer pressure smother the Word in you? Will you accept the Word until the love of riches and pleasure draw you away from it? Or will you accept the invitation to treasure the Word of God, allowing it to grow through careful nurturing until it bears fruit for others?

I invite you to explore your faith more deeply, to live your life more in tune with God's will, and to accept the salvation He offers through Christ and His church.

God be with you!

NOTES

CHAPTER ONE: The Purpose of Life
[1] *Catechism of the Catholic Church*, 356
[2] *Catechism of the Catholic Church*, 358
[3] Matthew 18:23-35
[4] Matthew 18:35
[5] Sirach 15:17

CHAPTER TWO: Where Should We Look for God
[1] Pope St. John Paul II, *Homily of John Paul II for the Canonization of Edith Stein*, Libreria Editrice Vaticana, Sunday, 11 October 1998, 3
[2] St. Catherine of Sienna, *The Dialogue of St. Catherine of Sienna*, TAN Books, 2010, 121
[3] *Catechism of the Catholic Church*, 230
[4] Michael Lipka, *American's Faith in God May be Eroding*, Pew Research Center, 4 November 2015
[5] Michael Coren, *Heresy, Ten Lies They Spread About Christians*, Signal Books, 2012, Ch 7
[6] Dr. Francis Collins, *Why This Scientist Believes in God*, CNN, 6 April 2007
[7] United States Conference of Catholic Bishops, *Biblical Novellas*, http://www.usccb.org/bible/scripture.cfm?src=_intros/novellas-intro.htm
[8] Pope Pius XII, *Humani Generis*, Libreria Editrice Vaticana, 12 August 1950, 36
[9] Matthew 5:30
[10] Amadeus, *The Truth Is Out There*, Catholic Answers, 2013, 26
[11] Amadeus, *The Truth Is Out There*, Catholic Answers, 2013, 26
[12] Damien Marsic, Mehran Sam, *DNA analysis of consecrated sacramental bread refutes Catholic transubstantiation claim*, Scientific Raelian, 25 October 2014

13 Rev. Peter M. J. Stravinskas et al., *Our Sunday Visitor's Catholic Dictionary*, Our Sunday Visitor Publishing Division, 1993, 472-473
14 Joan Carroll Cruz, *Eucharistic Miracles and Eucharistic Phenomena in the Lives of the Saints*, TAN Books, 1987, 3-7

CHAPTER THREE: What Separates Us From God
1 1 John 4:18
2 St. Catherine of Sienna, *The Dialogue of St. Catherine of Sienna*, TAN Books, 2010, 80
3 John 14:6
4 Malachi 3:6
5 Kenneth L. Woodward, *The Changing Face of the Church*, *Newsweek*, 15 April 2001
6 Saint Maria Faustina Kowalska, *Divine Mercy in My Soul, Diary of Saint Maria Faustina Kowalska*, Marian Press, 3rd edition with revisions 2011, 36
7 St. Catherine of Sienna, *The Dialogue of St. Catherine of Sienna*, TAN Books, 2010, pg. 22
8 Proverbs 10:2
9 Rev. Peter M. J. Stravinskas et al., *Our Sunday Visitor's Catholic Dictionary*, Our Sunday Visitor Publishing Division, 1993, 482
10 Catechism of the Catholic Church, 1855
11 Catechism of the Catholic Church, 1857
12 Catechism of the Catholic Church, 1856
13 Catechism of the Catholic Church, 1861
14 Catechism of the Catholic Church, 2181
15 Matthew 10:37
16 James 1:17
17 John 20:21-23

CHAPTER FOUR: Salvation
1 William A. Jurgens, *The Faith of the Early Fathers Volume 1*, The Liturgical Press, 1970, 767

[2] St. Catherine of Sienna, *The Dialogue of St. Catherine of Sienna,* TAN Books, 2010, 3-4

[3] Rev. Peter M. J. Stravinskas et al., *Our Sunday Visitor's Catholic Dictionary,* Our Sunday Visitor Publishing Division, 1993, 416

[4] St. Catherine of Sienna, *The Dialogue of St. Catherine of Sienna,* TAN Books, 2010, 152 – 153

[5] Saint Maria Faustina Kowalska, *Divine Mercy in My Soul, Diary of Saint Maria Faustina Kowalska,* Marian Press, 3rd edition with revisions 2011, 741

[6] Luke 16:19-31

[7] Mark 9:48

[8] Matthew 7:13

[9] 2 Peter 2:4

[10] St. John Bosco, *Forty Dreams of St. John Bosco From Saint John Bosco's Biographical Memoirs,* TAN Books, 2007, pg. 166

[11] John 14:2

[12] 1 Corinthians 2:9

[13] Revelation 21:3b-4

[14] 1 Timothy 2:3

[15] Luke 15:11-32

[16] Tim Staples, *Is Purgatory in the Bible?,* 17 January 2014, http://www.catholic.com/magazine/online-edition/is-purgatory-in-the-bible

[17] Philippians 2:12b

[18] Catechism of the Catholic Church, 330

[19] Matthew 7:21

CHAPTER FIVE: Love

[1] William A. Jurgens, *The Faith of the Early Fathers Volume 1,* The Liturgical Press, 1970, 433

[2] 1 John 4:8b

[3] Catechism of the Catholic Church, 733

[4] Matthew 22:37b-40

[5] Leviticus 19:18b

[6] Luke 12:6-7
[7] Jeremiah 1:5a
[8] John 14:15
[9] Rev. Peter M. J. Stravinskas et al., *Our Sunday Visitor's Catholic Dictionary*, Our Sunday Visitor Publishing Division, 1993, 311
[10] Isaiah 5:20a
[11] Proverbs 10:10
[12] 1 Corinthians 13:4:8a
[13] Matthew 7:3
[14] Saint Maria Faustina Kowalska, *Divine Mercy in My Soul, Diary of Saint Maria Faustina Kowalska*, Marian Press, 3rd edition with revisions 2011, 1103.
[15] John 15:18-19
[16] St. Augustine of Hippo, *The Confessions*, public domain, 400, Book 10.23.34.
[17] Matthew 5:44
[18] 1 John 4:20
[19] Luke 16:19-31

CHAPTER SIX: Mercy
[1] Matthew 20:1-16
[2] Charles G. Hebermann et al., *The Catholic Encyclopedia*, public domain, 1913, Presumption
[3] St. Catherine of Sienna, *The Dialogue of St. Catherine of Sienna*, TAN Books, 2010, 177
[4] Michael Day, *Pope Francis assures atheists: You don't have to believe in God to go to heaven*, The Independent, 11 September 2013
http://www.independent.co.uk/news/world/europe/pope-francis-assures-atheists-you-don-t-have-to-believe-in-god-to-go-to-heaven-8810062.html
[5] Jimmy Akin, Did Pope Francis Say That Atheists Can Get to Heaven by Good Works?, JimmyAkin.Com, 24 May 2013.

http://jimmyakin.com/2013/05/did-pope-francis-say-that-atheists-can-get-to-heaven-by-good-works.html

[6] United States Conference of Catholic Bishops, *Compendium of the Catechism of the Catholic Church*, Libreria Editrice Vaticana, 2006, 391

[7] John 8:11b

[8] 1 John 1:9

[9] Saint Maria Faustina Kowalska, *Divine Mercy in My Soul, Diary of Saint Maria Faustina Kowalska*, Marian Press, 3rd edition with revisions 2011, 1146

[10] Margaret Sanger, *Women and the New Race*, Public Domain, 1920, Chapter 5

[11] Pope Francis et al., *Beautiful Mercy*, Dynamic Catholic, 2015, 10

[12] Saint Maria Faustina Kowalska, *Divine Mercy in My Soul, Diary of Saint Maria Faustina Kowalska*, Marian Press, 3rd edition with revisions 2011, 1059

[13] Luke 7:40-50

[14] Luke 23:34b

[15] St. Catherine of Sienna, *The Dialogue of St. Catherine of Sienna*, TAN Books, 2010, 161

[16] St. Catherine of Sienna, *The Dialogue of St. Catherine of Sienna*, TAN Books, 2010, 160

[17] Hebrews 4:16

[18] Exodus 34:6

[19] Psalm 103:12

[20] Catechism of the Catholic Church, 1829

[21] Luke 6:36

[22] Matthew 18:22

[23] Matthew 5:7

[24] Matthew 25:40

[25] Saint Maria Faustina Kowalska, *Divine Mercy in My Soul, Diary of Saint Maria Faustina Kowalska*, Marian Press, 3rd edition with revisions 2011, 1148

[26] United States Conference of Catholic Bishops, *Compendium of the Catechism of the Catholic Church*, Libreria Editrice Vaticana, 2006, 193

[27] Sr. Marie Veritas et al., *Beautiful Mercy*, Dynamic Catholic, 2015, 81

[28] Ricardo Sanchez et al., The Quote Diary (Book Two), The New Americana, 55
https://www.quotev.com/story/4612828/The-Quote-Diary-Book-Two/55

CHAPTER SEVEN: Suffering

[1] Tyron Edwards, *A Dictionary of Thoughts: Being a Cyclopedia of Laconic Quotations From the Best Authors of the World, Both Ancient and Modern*, F. B. Dickerson Co, 1906, 583

[2] St. Catherine of Sienna, *The Dialogue of St. Catherine of Sienna*, TAN Books, 2010, 74

[3] Philippians 1:29

[4] 1 Peter 1:6-7

[5] St. Padre Pio, *Learning and Growing through Suffering*, Living with Christ, September 2008, 4

[6] Philippians 2:27

[7] Romans 8:17

[8] Georgina Molyneux, *The Cure D'Ars: A Memoir of Jean-Baptiste-Marie Vianney*, Richard Bentley Publisher, 1869, 123

[9] Luke 4:28-30

[10] John J. Delaney et al., *A Woman Clothed with the Sun – Eight Great Apparitions of Our Lady*, Doubleday, 1960, 172

[11] Sirach 2:4-5

CHAPTER EIGHT: Faith

[1] Hebrews 11:1-3

[2] Luke 12:29-31

[3] Mark 10:15

[4] Leviticus 19:31

[5] Catechism of the Catholic Church, 2116

[6] Matthew 7:7-8
[7] Exodus 4:13b
[8] Exodus 5:22-23
[9] Mark 4:35-41
[10] Matthew 14:28
[11] Matthew 14:31
[12] Matthew 26:69-75
[13] John 20:25b
[14] John 20:28-29
[15] Genesis 22:1-12
[16] Judges 7:1-25
[17] Mark 5:34
[18] Matthew 15:28
[19] Matthew 9:29-30a
[20] Matthew 8:13
[21] Acts 5:12-16
[22] Matthew 17:20
[23] Matthew 13:58
[24] 1 Corinthians 13:13
[25] 1 Corinthians 13:3
[26] James 2:24
[27] Matthew 18:5-6

CHAPTER NINE: Humility
[1] Rev. Peter M. J. Stravinskas et al., *Our Sunday Visitor's Catholic Dictionary*, Our Sunday Visitor Publishing Division, 1993, 257
[2] St. Catherine of Sienna, *The Dialogue of St. Catherine of Sienna*, TAN Books, 2010, 85.
[3] St. Catherine of Sienna, *The Dialogue of St. Catherine of Sienna*, TAN Books, 2010, 185.
[4] 1 Corinthians 3:7
[5] Philippians 4:13
[6] Peter Seewald, *Benedict XVI Last Testament in his own words*, Bloomsbury, 2016, 10

7 Saint Maria Faustina Kowalska, *Divine Mercy in My Soul, Diary of Saint Maria Faustina Kowalska*, Marian Press, 3rd edition with revisions 2011, 1563
8 1 John 1:8
9 Holly Taylor Coolman, *Summa 2.0*, America The National Catholic Review, August 4–11, 2014 Issue
10 Luke 3:16
11 Catechism of the Catholic Church, 470
12 Matthew 20:28a
13 Psalm 25:9
14 Matthew 8:8
15 Philippians 2:3
16 Catechism of the Catholic Church, 2559

CHAPTER TEN: Prayer
1 Genesis 3:9
2 2 Chronicles 7:14
3 Mark 11:24
4 1 Thessalonians 5:17
5 James 5:13-14
6 Catechism of the Catholic Church, 1
7 Catechism of the Catholic Church, 2626-2643
8 Rev. Peter M. J. Stravinskas et al., *Our Sunday Visitor's Catholic Dictionary*, Our Sunday Visitor Publishing Division, 1993, 101
9 Deuteronomy 9:25-26
10 1 Samuel 12:19
11 Job 42:10
12 James 5:16
13 Ephesians 6:19-20
14 1 Timothy 2:1
15 Luke 17:17
16 1 Thessalonians 5:18
17 Catechism of the Catholic Church, 2639
18 Catechism of the Catholic Church, 2705

[19] Luke 11:5-13 & Luke 18:1-8
[20] Luke 22:42

CHAPTER ELEVEN: Hope
[1] Catechism of the Catholic Church, 1817
[2] William A. Jurgens, *The Faith of the Early Fathers Volume 2*, The Liturgical Press, 1979, 1312
[3] Isaiah 40:8
[4] Acts 17:28
[5] William A. Jurgens, *The Faith of the Early Fathers Volume 1*, The Liturgical Press, 1970, 836
[6] Matthew 25:14-30
[7] 1 Corinthians 12:4-7
[8] Matthew 5:14-16
[9] Mark 4:3-10, 13-20

Stephen Reidy is a life-long Catholic who lives with his wife and three sons in central Massachusetts. He's served the church as an altar server, usher, lector, and religious education teacher. He earned a Bachelor of Science degree in business administration from the University of Massachusetts, Lowell, and an MBA from Bentley University. He also honorably served six years in the Army National Guard. His spiritual life is rooted in the Eucharist, prayer, and the reading of Scripture and the works of the saints.

Made in the USA
Lexington, KY
16 December 2017